HOW
TO
EAT
AN
ELEPHANT

The What, Why, and How of the Bible

JOSH GREEN

LUCIDBOOKS

To my wife, Callie,
for always believing in me even before I do.
You're my best friend forever.

CONTENTS

SPECIAL THANKS

I would not have been able to write this book without the encouragement of my wife Callie. For several years she urged me to put this content into book form, and I resisted. I am so honored that she loves me, supports me, and pushes me further than I ever dreamed.

To my Thursday accountability group (in order of importance . . . just kidding)—Jason Cave, Connor Cook, Hunter Cox, Randy Green, and Josh Liles—you guys read early drafts of the book and gave incredibly valuable insights and edits. Not only that, but you provide a space for me to be just a normal disciple. I don't have to wear the pastor hat around you guys. I have been able to be personally known and grow tremendously because you all have loved me well.

Lastly, thank you to Colonial Hill Baptist Church. I have never met a more generous church who loves their staff so well. It is an honor to serve!

INTRODUCTION

I am the product of several generations of faith. In my family tree is a lot of brokenness, like in all families, but my two grandmothers are giants in the faith. I believe I am reaping the benefits of their faith being passed down from generation to generation.

I grew up in the church. It was a more traditional church setting, which meant I was at church Sunday mornings (for Sunday school and the worship hour), Sunday nights, and Wednesday nights. I heard a pastor once say, "I grew up with a drug problem. I was drug to church every time the doors were open." I can say the exact same thing.

My grandparents and parents grew up in churches that centered on the Word of God. The churches I grew up in had a very high view of the Bible. I remember sitting through many church services where I had no idea what was going on, but my parents had their Bibles on their laps. I remember thumbing through the pages and seeing some words in black and some in red. I remember the smell of the soft pages and how they began to come to life when I started reading the Word for myself in my sophomore year of high school.

I am proud of the fact that my upbringing rooted me in the Bible. In my ministry and my family, I have tried to carry on this same high view of the Word of God.

What you hold in your hands has been gathered and compiled over 20 years of my ministry and life. I want to help people see the beauty, depth, and hope found in the Bible. It is fascinating, beautiful, and true.

Most of all, I hope this book helps those who may be younger in their faith speed up their ability to grasp the Book that is essential to their faith. I don't want people just to grasp what the Bible contains. My heart's desire is that they would learn how to read it so they might connect deeply with the Creator of the universe.

When I first began reading and attempting to grasp the Bible, it felt overwhelming. It felt daunting to think I could comprehend the contents of the entire collection of 66 books. That is why the title of this book is *How to Eat an Elephant*. Eating an elephant is nearly impossible. But if you do eat an elephant, there is only one way to do it—one bite at a time. If you want to grasp the contents of the Word of God, there is only one way to do it—continue to chip away over and over.

If you consistently immerse yourself in the Word of God, there may be times when you don't feel like you are growing or grasping the information. As you look back over a long period of time after applying the principles laid out in this book, you will see that God was growing you and changing you all along the way. Your goal today isn't to know the whole Bible. Your goal today is to faithfully take steps of faith and run the race that God has set before you. I pray this book helps you do just that.

- Chapter 1 gives a basic foundation of the Bible and shows how God is the main character.

- Chapter 2 deals with inspiration and preservation to help people build confidence to trust the Word of God.

- Chapters 3–6 tell the one, big, overarching story of the Bible. Chapter 3 deals with God's creation and the introduction of sin into the world. Chapter 4 walks you through the book of Genesis to set the stage for the rest of the story. Chapter 5 teaches the high points of the story from Exodus to Malachi (the rest of the Old Testament). Chapter 6 tells us how Jesus is the hero. It explains the gospel and how the whole Bible is about Jesus.

- Chapter 7 shows us how to read the Bible in such a way that we actually commune with the living God. Chapter 8 includes questions to ask and tools to help you study more deeply.

In today's culture, biblical illiteracy has become the norm—but it doesn't have to stay that way. This book was written to help change that. Each chapter includes Small Group

Questions, making it an ideal resource for youth groups, small groups, and even church-wide studies. Whether used individually or in community, it's designed to help believers build a solid, lasting foundation in God's Word.

You can read this book straight through or one chapter at a time. Each chapter stands alone and is helpful in its own way. But ultimately, I hope this book helps you understand the Book so you might know Him.

In Christ,
Josh Green

Chapter 1

FOUNDATIONS

God is the main character of the Bible, not us. To misunderstand this is to misread the Bible. That doesn't mean the Bible isn't for us. It overwhelmingly is. In fact, God being the main character of the Bible is the best news we could imagine.

Why would I start a book with that first paragraph? In all my years (decades) of ministry, no one has ever asked me who the main character of the Bible is. I think it is because most of us don't think of the Bible in those terms. The average Christian treats the Bible like a rule book. They assume that it tells them what they should and should not do. There are also some miracles, stories, and unexplainable things in the Bible. Overall, the normal Christian attending church on a Sunday morning assumes the Bible is a how-to manual.

It is so much better than that.

> *God is the main character of the Bible, not us.*

God

Before we can get into the details of the Bible, we must start with God Himself. Why? Because the Bible starts with God. The very first verse in the Bible says, "In the beginning God created the heavens and the earth" (Gen. 1:1).

The Bible never attempts to prove the existence of God. It assumes the reality that everything we see and experience ultimately points to our Creator God. There is a divine Creator. That is why there is order in the world. That is why the world works. That is why life is possible. God logically designed and ordered the universe to work.

At the heart of everything in this book is a deep conviction that the Bible is about God first and foremost. That means God is not only the main character but also the hero. From the beginning of the book to the end, it is a book about God.

Ultimately, the story of the Bible (and of the world) is one grand story about God. I'll explain that in Chapter 3.

Misplaced Worldview

It is important to start with God because the temptation is always to focus on ourselves. By the way, that is sin—the constant desire to put ourselves first and assume the world revolves around us. Please allow me to get on my soapbox for a minute. I promise it will make sense in the end.

In our modern era, people assume the Bible is about them. Because of that, they expect the church to cater to them. Many also fail to grasp the reality that the church is a people called by God, bound together in community to do life and pursue the mission of God. People sometimes struggle to fully involve themselves in the life of the church because they have been trained that "me" is more important than "we." This misunderstanding leads us to miss much of God's blessing and how He intends to use us and grow us.

In case you disagree, let me attempt to prove it. We live in a world where everything exists to serve us and make us the focal point. Almost everything in your life can be customized to exactly what you want when you want it. We all have cell phones, but the organization of our phones, what apps we have, and where they are located are vastly different.

Social media is tailored to us. The algorithms learn your habits, know what videos you share or watch, and recognize the type of content you interact with the most. Then you get more of that content for your viewing pleasure. Their hope is that you spend more time on their platform because what you are seeing is tailored to your preferences and desires. The more time you spend on their platform is how they determine success, and that generates more income for them.

This individualistic worldview isn't necessarily bad or sinful, but it can be. If we truly see ourselves, our wants, our desires, and our needs as most important to our existence, then much of the Bible and our experience with God's church will not make sense. Our culture has trained us to view the world with ourselves at the very center. The biggest problem with that idea is that we love it. I love it. I love it when I am the focal point, and all my needs are being met. I love it when I get exactly what I want when I want it. You do too. But biblically, we are made for something far greater and more impactful than the limited view of glorifying ourselves.

When you make yourself the primary point of the Bible, you will inevitably veer off God's path. You will be tempted to make the Bible say and mean things about you that it doesn't say or mean. The typical result of this view is that it reduces God to a genie in a bottle. It leads us to believe that God exists to make us happy and cater to our needs. This is an unhealthy and false way to read and understand the story of the world.

When this individualistic worldview bleeds into the modern church and the way we understand the Bible, the temptation is to tailor the weekend church "experience" to perceived needs so more and more people will attend. I am all for pursuing excellence in all things because our God deserves our excellence. I also believe that people should *want* to be at church because it is done well, it is fun and

> *When you make yourself the primary point of the Bible, you will inevitably veer off God's path.*

engaging, and it is beneficial for them. But that does not mean that we are the center or focal point. It is so easy to shift from a God-centered perspective to a human-centered perspective in the church because it gives us certain results. What is most helpful and beneficial for humankind is to have a very high view of God and make Him the focal point of our lives and our worship experiences.

The proper view of the Bible is a God-centered view. That

means the main character of the Bible is God (Luke 24:27). Ultimately, the story of the Bible is God's story, and we have the privilege to play a part.

Because our culture has trained us in an individualistic way, it is only natural that we expect our religious experiences to fit into this mold. I am not saying that you will go to hell if you take this individualistic worldview. But I am saying that if you make yourself the focal point of the Bible, you will miss the depth, beauty, and satisfaction of having a proper view of the God of the universe.

Is the Bible a Road Map?

I have heard many people, pastors included, refer to the Bible as the road map for life. I understand what they are trying to communicate, but I think it is also misleading.

> *The proper view of the Bible is a God-centered view.*

When I use my GPS, it tells me exactly what turns to make and when. It tells me how long I have before the next turn. It even gives me an ETA, which I consider a challenge to beat with everything in my power, which may a problem.

The Bible does not direct our lives like this, but many times we try to use it that way. This line of thinking makes it seem like the point of the Bible is just to tell us what to do. If you have this problem, read this verse. If you want a good life, do this. If you are struggling here, try this. The Bible isn't a tool for a quick fix to our lives. It is so much more and so much better.

What if the Bible were written differently than this? What if we understood what the Bible really is so we know how to read it in a way that is more helpful and beneficial? What if God has different goals for our Bible reading than we understand? This book is written to help us more fully think through what the Bible is and how we interact with it on a daily basis.

Who Is the Bible For?

Here is another potentially controversial sentence: The Bible is not written to us. If that feels controversial, hear me out. The Bible is not written to us in the way we might think.

I married my wife in 2005. I didn't have a Bible verse that told me, "Josh, marry Callie in 2005." I don't have verses that told me to close the church I was pastoring and move back to my hometown of Snyder, Texas, in 2019. I am completely convinced that both of those things were from God and were His exact will and purpose for my life, but I didn't have a verse that told me to do those things.

That is because the Bible is not written *to us*; it is written *for us*. The Bible does more than tell us what to do; it teaches us who to be. It does tell us to do and not do certain things, but overwhelmingly, it teaches us the kind of people God has created us to be.

As we begin to learn to read the Bible together, there will be many times when you have no idea what you are supposed to "do" after reading a certain text. It's fiiiine (inside joke—love all you at Colonial Hill). Deeper than learning what to do, we understand that in reading the Bible, God is

> *The Bible is not written to us; it is written for us.*

teaching us who to be. As it turns out, that is way better than just getting answers to every single question we have.

The Bottom Line

Here is what the Bible really is. It is the primary way God has chosen to reveal Himself to mankind. I did not say the only way. I said the primary way. God has primarily given us His Word so we might know Him (more on this in Chapter 2).

We will dive into this fully later, but the goal of reading the Bible isn't to read the Bible. The goal for the Christian is to commune with the living God. Because the Bible is the primary way God has chosen to reveal Himself to us, we read the Bible because it leads us to the heart of God.

In John 5, Jesus is arguing with some religious leaders and makes a statement that is very fascinating and formative for our discussion. He says in John 5:39–40, "You study the Scriptures diligently because you think that in them you

> *The Bible is the primary way God has chosen to reveal Himself to mankind.*

have eternal life. These are the very Scriptures that testify about me, yet you refuse to come to me to have life."

This is fascinating because I would love to have a church full of people who are diligently studying the Bible. But what if our study of the Bible is missing the point of studying the Bible?

We do not worship the Bible. We worship the God of the Bible. The reason God gave us the Bible is because it leads us to Him.

When we spend time devotionally reading the Bible, we are attempting to commune with the living God who has chosen to reveal Himself through His Word. That allows us to know His nature and character. We see His justice and mercy. We see His wrath and indignation. We see His love and compassion. We see what He loves and hates. And the more we learn about the God of the universe, the more power it has to change us and transform us.

Paul said it like this in 2 Corinthians 3:18: "And we all, who with unveiled faces contemplate the Lord's glory, are being transformed into his image with ever-increasing glory, which comes from the Lord, who is the Spirit." As we read the Word of God and are confronted with the nature and character of God, it shapes and

> *We do not worship the Bible. We worship the God of the Bible.*

forms us more and more into God's image. As we read and submit to the Word, God shapes us, corrects us, encourages us, and so much more.

Guess what? If you hate to read, you still need to have your head and heart saturated with the Word of God. We do not read the Bible because we love reading. We read the Bible because it connects us with the heart of our Creator, and we were made for that kind of connection. I promise, the Bible is better than you can imagine.

When we get into the big story (metanarrative), we'll see two major themes. One is that mankind is sinful. We aren't just sinful; we are more sinful than we want to admit. This sinfulness isn't like a scratch on the arm that needs a Band-Aid. This sinfulness is a brokenness in our core. It is so deep and pervasive that we cannot fix it ourselves. The second theme that runs through the story is the lengths God is willing to go to rescue and redeem mankind.

The Bible really is the story of God who saves, heals, and restores. He does this because it allows Him to show off His glory and His nature, but also because His intent

> *God is the main character.*
> *Jesus is the hero.*

and design is for us to know Him. He will do everything necessary so mankind can come back into a perfect relationship with the Father.

God is the main character. Jesus is the hero. The Holy Spirit empowers it all. We are saved, redeemed, and restored even though we don't deserve it. God gets all the glory. It is the best news possible, and I can't wait to walk you through the whole story in detail.

But before we get to the big story, how did we get the Bible in the first place? The next chapter helps us wrap our minds around that question.

SMALL GROUP QUESTIONS

1. Before reading this chapter, what was your view of the Bible? How did this chapter help you form a more biblical view?

2. In what ways do you find yourself expecting the church to cater to your personal wants or preferences? How can preferences be both helpful and harmful?

3. The chapter said, "The Bible is not written *to us*; it is written *for us*." Explain this in your own words.

4. How would it be possible to worship the Bible and not the God of the Bible? Have you ever seen this in real life?

5. What do you think this means: "Jesus is the hero"?

Chapter 2

WHY CAN WE TRUST
THE BIBLE?

Judge me if you want, but I enjoy listening to Joe Rogan's pod-cast, *The Joe Rogan Experience*. The language is colorful, and the subject matter is typically adult. One of the main reasons I listen to it is because Joe and I have different views of the world. His opinions differ from many of mine, and that challenges me to know what I believe and why.

Often Joe Rogan talks about religions or the Bible. He says that the Bible started as verbal stories told from generation to generation. What he is almost always getting at is that this is one reason the Bible can't be trusted. When stories are passed from person to person, they almost always lose significant details and meaning.

It's like playing "telephone," a game I played as a kid. You start with one sentence and secretly whisper that to the first person. "A bunch of yellow bananas launched on a blue boat."

Then they whisper the same sentence to the next person. It goes all the way down the line, and then the last person is supposed to say the original sentence out loud. The last player in the game might say, "The sentence is 'Orange buses drive into the boat ramp.'" I have never seen this game played successfully. It's hilarious to see how it morphs.

Many people, seemingly Joe Rogan included, logically deduce that because the Bible began as stories verbally passed from person to person, we can't possibly trust that the stories are accurate.

What if the Bible was actually preserved by an Almighty God? That would drastically change the outcome and the validity of what we have.

How Did We Get the Bible?

If I were to ask you who wrote the Bible, what would you say? Most people would say people in history. That is actually true. Kings, prophets, fishermen, and others wrote the words we have. That leads us to another question. If such a random group of people wrote such a big book, how can it be trusted? I am glad you asked.

We believe that this book was written by men but through the inspiration of God Himself. I have heard other pastors say it like this: God wrote the Bible, but men held the pen. Even though God used people, ultimately God is the author.

We believe that the Bible is literally breathed out by God.

Second Timothy 3:16–17 says, "All Scripture is God-breathed and is useful for teaching, rebuking, correcting and training in right- eousness, so that the servant of

> *God wrote the Bible, but men held the pen.*

God may be thoroughly equipped for every good work." Sec- ond Peter 1:21 says, "For prophecy never had its origin in the human will, but prophets, though human, spoke from God as they were carried along by the Holy Spirit."

So yes, humans wrote the Bible, but they were under the inspiration of God Himself. Ultimately, that means God wrote the Bible and just used humans to do it. That is called divine inspiration, which creates a massive amount of encouragement for believers. Left to themselves, humans could never have pro- duced the Bible. But if the God who spoke creation into exist- ence is the author, it seems pretty simple for Him to preserve what He wrote.

The fact that 10 people can't get one sentence right in the game of telephone, but we have this Bible in our hands is a great comfort to me. It reinforces the truth that this is written by God, not humans.

Try to imagine humans writing the Bible when the Bible is written in three languages. The Old Testament is written in Hebrew. The New Testament is mostly written in Greek, but some of it is in Aramaic.

The Bible was written over the course of about 1,500 years and has over 40 human authors.[1] They wrote on three conti- nents—Asia, Africa, and Europe.

The Bible is a collection of 66 books. There are 39 books in the Old Testament and 27 in the New Testament.

"The human authors of the Bible include kings, peasants, philosophers, fishermen, poets, statements, a doctor, and scholars. The books of the Bible cover history, sermons, letters, songs, and love letters. There are geographical surveys, architectural specifications, travel diaries, population statistics, family tress, inventories, and numerous legal documents."[2]

The 66 books also have various writing styles. There are historical accounts, stories, sermons, letters, poems, songs, genealogical lists, and more.

Here is the most incredible thing. Even though the Bible was written over 1,500 years on three continents by all kinds of people, it is still unified and without contradiction. The Bible tells one overarching story about the lengths God is willing to go to rescue and redeem a sinful people so they might know Him and enjoy Him for all eternity.

> *The Bible tells one overarching story about the lengths God is willing to go to rescue and redeem a sinful people so they might know Him and enjoy Him for all eternity.*

All these people could not do this by themselves. The actual author of the Bible is God Himself.

Preservation

Someone may push back and say, "You are just giving facts about the Bible. How can we even trust that what we have today has been preserved?" How do we know that the Bible we have in our hand is what was written all those years ago? Let me explain.

We don't have any original manuscripts of the Bible. We don't have the actual letter Paul wrote to Timothy where he wrote the words in 2 Timothy 3:16–17. But we do have thousands of copies and fragments of the Bible. If that doesn't make sense, hang on because I am about to nerd out about this. This is as simple as I can make it. If you want more detail about this subject, I encourage you to look at Wesley Huff's website.

We have many manuscript copies and fragments that we can compare to each other. Because of that, we can be very confident that God has preserved His Word for us. The Bible has been meticulously copied and compared over the years so we can be confident that what we have is the Word that was written all those years ago.

When I say *copied*, I don't mean some random person taking notes about something they remembered. Biblical transmission was nothing like that. The printing press was not invented until the 15th century, so Holy Scripture had to be copied by hand. Scribes were professional copiers. Each letter in ancient Hebrew was written in rows and columns like a grid. Scribes copied the Old Testament Scriptures meticulously, letter by letter, line by line. Thus, the job of a scribe was not a child's game; it was a sacred duty.

So how can we possibly know our Bibles are correct? Imagine for a moment that the original copy of the United States Constitution was destroyed in a fire. Does that mean the exact wording is lost forever? No.

Think about how many copies have been made of the Constitution over time, whether they are printed copies or reproduced in books. There are so many copies to compare that even if we lost the original Constitution, we can know with confidence what the original said.

The same is true of the Bible. Just to be clear, we are not talking about whether or not the Bible is true. By the end of the chapter, I hope to show you why it is trustworthy. For now, I want to show you how we can be confident that what we have today is what was originally written.

When discussing the reliability of any ancient text, there are three factors to bear in mind:

1. When it was originally written
2. The date of the oldest copy
3. The number of copies

Before examining the Bible, let's look at other works of antiquity. I am including three examples, but you can find many others if you do an online search. We have no originals of these works, but look at the details regarding their writing, preservation, and accuracy.

- Tacitus is one of the most important ancient Roman historians. He lived from AD 56–120 and wrote *Annals*, which concern Rome from AD 14–68. There are 36 manuscripts, the earliest from AD 850. So there are over 800 years between the original writing and the manuscript copy that we have.

- Julius Caesar's cataloguing of the Gallic Wars was composed from 58–50 BC. There are about 250 known manuscripts, but only nine or 10 are in good condition. The oldest manuscript is about 900 years after Julius Caesar's time period.

- Homer lived around 900 BC. The earliest copies of his famous works *The Iliad* and *The Odyssey* date around 415 BC, giving a time span of nearly 500 years. There are over 1,900 ancient copies of his work.[3]

Keep in mind that scholars generally accept the reliability and authenticity of these ancient works. Have you ever heard someone argue that we can't trust *The Iliad* we have today because we do not have the original that Homer wrote? No, you haven't because all the ancient texts I referred to are accepted as accurate.

So what about the New Testament?

- The New Testament was written from AD 40–100, and the earliest existing fragment is from roughly AD 125. That is a difference of about 25 years between when it was written and the earliest copy.

There are over 24,000 copies and fragments of manuscripts.[4]

Not only do we have an overwhelming number of manuscripts and fragments, but when we compare them to each other, here are the results:

- There is about 95 percent agreement among all the manuscripts.

- Most of the variances are due to spelling and punctuation differences.

- Not one major Christian doctrine is impacted by any manuscript variances.

To put it more clearly, if there are contradictions or differences in the manuscripts that are being compared, the contradictions are not like "This one says Jesus rose from the dead, and this one says Jesus did *not* rise from the dead." Those are not the issues we find when we compare manuscripts. Most issues are something like there's a comma in this one and not in that one. No issue with the manuscripts impacts any major doctrine we believe.

> *Not one major Christian doctrine is impacted by any manuscript variances.*

We can be highly confident that the Bible we have today matches what was originally written. It can be trusted because God has preserved it and wants His people to have His Word.

Probability

What we've covered is convincing, but that isn't even the most convincing. Did you know that the Messiah, Jesus, fulfilled over 300 prophecies that were predicted about Him in the Old Testament? That is crazy! What is even crazier is that so many were outside of Jesus's control.

Peter W. Stoner and Robert C. Newman wrote a book in 1958 called *Science Speaks*.[5] Stoner was a mathematics professor and applied the science of probability to the Scriptures in regard to prophecies concerning the Messiah.

He looked at eight of more than 300 prophecies in the Old Testament.[6]

Below are those eight prophecies.

1. The time of Jesus's birth, prophesied in Daniel 8–9 approximately 530 years before Jesus's birth.

2. Jesus would be born in Bethlehem, prophesied in Micah 5:2 approximately 700 years before it happened.

3. The Messiah would be born of a virgin, prophesied in Isaiah 7:14 approximately 700 years before it happened.

4. Jesus would be betrayed for 30 pieces of silver, prophesied in Zechariah 11:12 approximately 500 years before it happened.

5. Jesus would be mocked, prophesied in Psalm 22:7–8 approximately 1,000 years before it happened.

6. Jesus would be crucified, prophesied in John 3:14 approximately one to three years before it happened.

7. Jesus would be pierced, prophesied in Psalms 22:16 approximately 1,000 years before it happened.

8. Jesus would die with the wicked, but He would be buried with the rich, prophesied in Isaiah 53:9 approximately 700 years before it happened.

Stoner attempted to answer this question: "What is the probability that one man could fulfill these eight prophesies?" Again, most of them were out of Jesus's control. Working with his students at Westmont College, Stoner conservatively determined that the probability of one man fulfilling these eight prophesies is one in 10^{17}. That is one person in a number with 17 zeros. We don't even have a name for that big of a number.

To illustrate how large the number 10^{17} is, Stoner gave an illustration. Suppose we take 10^{17} silver dollars and lay them on the state of Texas. They'll cover the entire state 2 feet deep. Now mark one of those silver dollars and stir the whole mass thoroughly all over the state. Blindfold a person, tell them they can travel as far as they wish but must pick up only one silver dollar. What chance would they have of getting the marked silver dollar?

They would have the same chance the prophets had to write these eight prophecies and have them all come true for any one man from their day to the present time.

Stoner did another study with 48 prophecies instead of eight. The extremely conservative probability of one person fulfilling all 48 prophecies is 10^{157}. That number is 10 with 157 zeroes. That is a conservative probability that Jesus fulfilled all 48 prophecies. And Jesus fulfilled over 300 prophecies. This is staggering!

Old Testament and New Testament Canonization

I hope this is building your faith and confidence in God and His Word. Here is another question we should explore. How can we trust that the 66 books that comprise the Bible are the books that are supposed to be included and that no books were accidentally left out?

Have you ever heard someone refer to the Apocrypha, the Gospel of Thomas, or the Gospel of Judas? Why are they not included in the Bible, but the Gospel of Matthew is? That can be a very weighty subject, but here is a simple overview. I will also provide a few resources if you want to learn more.

Here is a nerdy definition. The biblical canon is the collection of scriptural books that God has given His corporate people and are distinguished by their divine qualities, reception by the collective body, and their apostolic connection either by authorship or association.[7]

In English, the biblical canon is the group of books that have met the proper criteria for being accepted as divinely inspired by God.

Old Testament

For the 39 books of the Old Testament, there is little to no dispute about whether or not they should be included. In fact, in the time of Jesus during the first century, the entirety of the Old Testament that we have was considered divinely inspired by God. Even Josephus, a secular scholar, says in regard to the Old Testament, "For although such long ages have now passed, no one has ventured neither to add, or to remove, or to alter a syllable."[8]

> *The biblical canon is the group of books that have met the proper criteria for being accepted as divinely inspired by God.*

Jesus viewed the Old Testament as divinely inspired Scripture. He constantly quoted the Old Testament. In the Gospels, Jesus taught this about the Old Testament:

- It is the Word of God (Mark 7:13) and the commandment of God (Matt. 15:3).

- It could not be broken (John 10:35) or destroyed (Matt. 5:18).

- It is truth (John 17:17).

- It is sufficient for faith and holy living (Luke 16:31).

Jesus relied on the Old Testament for authority and knowledge whether He was being questioned by His disciples (Matt. 21:16), tested by the Pharisees (Matt. 12:3, 22:29), or tempted by Satan (Matt. 4:1–11).

Jesus not only confirmed Old Testament teachings as authoritative and binding but also referred to the following people and events, proving their historical validity:

- God's creation of the world (Mark 13:19)
- A literal Adam and Eve (Matt. 19:4–5)
- Cain murdering his brother, Abel (Luke 11:51)
- Noah and the ark (Matt. 24:37–38)
- The life and faith of Abraham (John 8:56)
- Jonah and the great fish (Matt. 12:40)
- The destruction of Sodom and Gomorrah and the death of Lot's wife (Luke 17:29, 32)
- Moses and the burning bush (Mark 12:26)
- The manna provided to the Israelites in the wilderness (John 6:31–51)

It is clear that Jesus thought the Old Testament was accurate and authoritative. Again, in the first century during Jesus's time, the Old Testament was not in dispute.

New Testament

The Old Testament is rarely disputed, but the New Testament has been criticized throughout the years. How did we settle on the 27 books of the New Testament?

Scholars and leaders in the church had some criteria to help decide which writings were divinely inspired and which were not. Simply put, the New Testament went through these three criteria:

- The writing must be biblical. It cannot contradict God's Word in the Old Testament. It had to be in line with the teachings already established as divinely inspired.

- The writings must be authoritative, a quality that deals with writing directly from Jesus's apostles. The apostles walked with Jesus and gave firsthand accounts. Many of their writings were inspired by the Holy Spirit as the Word of God. There are some authors who were not Jesus's apostles, but they had firsthand conversations with the apostles who taught them what Jesus said.

- The writings must have a corporate reception among church leadership. That means they are widespread and widely accepted by the church as authoritative and accurate. One person or sect did not say these writings should be accepted as divine inspiration. The writings were widely accepted by God's people as being divinely inspired by God Himself.[9]

By the second century, 22 of the 27 books of the New Testament seem to be functioning as Scripture by the church. Those core books were the four Gospels, Acts, the 13 epistles of Paul, Hebrews, 1 Peter, 1 John, and Revelation. Books that were disputed tended to be smaller books such as 2 Peter, Jude, James, 2 John, and 3 John.[10]

In the fourth century through a series of church councils and debates, the full 27 books of the New Testament were officially canonized. That means they were officially recognized by the church as authoritative and the divinely inspired Word of God. Those 27 books are the books of the New Testament the church recognizes today.

Conclusion

I am aware that we just covered a lot of technical information. My heart is to help build trust in the Word of God. The book we have is not an accident. It has not been mishandled. God not only wrote and authored every word but also preserved them because He wants us to know Him. What a privilege we have!

The Bible is the primary way God has chosen to reveal Himself. Because He has revealed Himself, we have knowledge of the truth. And as we continue to learn about the Word of God, you will see the beauty in those pages and the incredible invitation of God to His people through His Word.

---------- SMALL GROUP QUESTIONS ----------

1. How would you explain inspiration (see the second paragraph of the section "How Did We Get the Bible?")?

2. In the "How Did We Get the Bible?" section are facts about the authorship of the Bible and its contents. Which of these details stood out to you the most? Why?

3. Did the "Preservation" section help build your confidence in trusting God's Word? Why or why not?

4. Write the number 10 with 17 zeros (from the section "Probability"). Make up a word for that big of a number.

5. What are the implications if Christians cannot trust the Bible? What are the implications if the Bible is fully trustworthy?

Chapter 3

WHAT IS THE BIBLE ABOUT?

Metanarrative Part 1:
The Bad News

What I am attempting to show you has been revolutionary for me, and I think it will help a lot of people. When I first began digging into the Word, I found a verse here or a paragraph there that spoke to whatever I was struggling with. If I was struggling with anxiety, I read Philippians 4:4–7. If I was struggling with lust, I went to Psalm 51 or Proverbs 7. If I was struggling with anger, James 1:19–20 was so helpful.

Hear me. This is not wrong, but there is a fuller way to read and understand the Bible. That is what I will to show you in the next four chapters.

What if the Bible was not primarily designed for you to pick and choose a random verse? What if the Bible was really one big story with a lot of depth, meaning, and hope? What if understanding the whole story made each individual verse or paragraph mean so much more?

I am going to walk you through the overarching story of the Bible from Genesis to Revelation. That is called the metanarrative, or big story. It is a 30,000-foot view. Every story you have ever heard about the Bible fits into God's grand story. You as a believer are in the middle of this massive story of God.

This can be overwhelming. That is why I called this book *How to Eat an Elephant.* It can feel like you will never grasp all this information, but I promise that you can. If I can learn this, you can too.

Remember from Chapter 1 that God is the main character of the Bible. The Bible is one big story of the lengths God is willing to go to rescue and redeem mankind. It can be broken up into four major sections: Creation, Fall, Redemption, and Restoration. We will cover Creation and Fall in this chapter.

Creation: Genesis 1-2

The story begins with creation in Genesis 1–2. God creates the world and speaks everything into existence. He creates everything good. There is rhythm, order, and perfection. These are days 1–5.

> *Creation, Fall, Redemption, and Restoration*

Have you ever considered how incredibly creative our God is? He created the sun, the moon, and the stars. He created all kind of animals, insects, and birds. He created millions of different creatures that live in the waters. He created mountains, beaches, and forests.

Life works because God made it possible to work. The ecosystems function because God designed them that way. Science can be science, and math can be math because God logically made the world the way it is.

God's creation is good, and it is made by a good God. Books are constantly written detailing how marvelous this world is. Even though days 1–5 are fascinating, day 6 is even better.

Day 6 is different than the first five days. On this day, God forms male and female humans and breathes life into their nostrils. Not only are they intimately formed but they are different than the rest of what God had already created. Unlike anything else, humans are made in God's image and given responsibility and dominion over the rest of creation (Genesis 1:26–27).

Being made in the image of God is called the *Imago Dei*, which is significant to understand life and purpose. No other animal has inherent reason, logic, and intuition like humans do. Humans have value, dignity, and worth because they are made in the image of God.

We are created to rule and have dominion over the rest of creation. Adam and Eve had work and purpose. All of God's creation is good, but humanity is very good.

Most importantly, the *Imago Dei* gives humans a unique ability to connect with God. In His goodness, God created humans so they might know Him and walk with Him all their days. This is God's heart. He is good and desires His creation to know Him.

On day 7, God rested.

Genesis 1 and 2 show us how God intended life to be lived. The Garden of Eden was a place of peace, joy, and purity. There was meaningful work and rest. There was marriage and sexual relations. Overall, life was marked by harmony among humans and what was created and harmony with humans and God. We must see God's heart and intentions. This is real, pure life. We must grasp these ideas in order for the rest of the story to make sense.

But everything changes in Genesis 3 when sin enters the world.

Fall: Genesis 3

Adam and Eve are in the Garden of Eden, and God has given them specific commands about what they can and cannot do. Genesis 2:15–17 says, "The Lord God took the man and put him in the Garden of Eden to work it and take care of it. And the Lord God commanded the man, 'You are free to eat from any tree in the garden; but you must not eat from the tree of the knowledge of good and evil, for when you eat from it you will certainly die.'"

The command from God is that Adam and Eve are free to do anything they can imagine except eat from one tree, the tree of the knowledge of good and evil. Think about the freedom they had to enjoy all of life. They had meaningful work and rest, play, friendship, good food, intimacy, and so much more. They only had one rule. One!

If this were a movie, Genesis 1 and 2 would be the opening scenes where there is life, joy, and excitement. There is happiness. Life is great. As Genesis 3 opens, the music in the background of the movie would become more sinister. We would be introduced to Satan, the serpent.

The audience would be on the edge of their seats because we know this enemy is trying to destroy all that God created that was good. How will Adam and Eve respond when the enemy shows himself? Watch what happens.

Now the serpent was more crafty than any of the wild animals the Lord God had made. He said to the woman, "Did God really say, 'You must not eat from any tree in the garden'?" The woman said to the serpent, "We may eat fruit from the trees in the garden, but God did say, 'You must not eat fruit from the tree that is in the middle of the garden, and you must not touch it, or you will die.'" "You will not certainly die," the serpent said to the woman. "For God knows that when you eat from it your eyes will be opened, and you will be like God, knowing good and evil." When the woman saw that the fruit of the tree was good for food and pleasing to the eye, and also desirable for gaining wisdom, she took some and ate it.

—Gen. 3:1–6

Remember, Adam and Eve can do anything except eat from one tree. When Satan begins to talk with Eve, he deceives and lies. He does not tell the whole truth. He hints that maybe God is withholding something from them. "Did God really say . . . ?" God's command is to not eat it. Eve says that she can't even touch it, or she will die.

In this moment, Adam and Eve are both forced to make a decision about whether or not they will believe and trust what God said.

The music in this scene would be climactic because Genesis 3 radically changes the direction of the world. Adam and Eve are in the Garden, and everything is perfect. When sin enters the world, all that God created good is now broken and fractured.

Sin

We have to pause here and talk about sin more thoroughly. The more we understand sin the way the Bible talks about sin, the more the story makes sense. If we have a low view of sin, then the story isn't really that big of a deal. How does the Bible describe sin?

Surveying the Bible, we see that sin is vastly deeper than we tend to assume. Sin is a failure to honor God in thought, word, deed, or motive. But what does that really mean? Let's try to wrap our minds around what the Bible teaches.

Our sin is first and foremost a heart condition. When I say heart, I am obviously not talking about the organ in your body.

I am talking about your inward person—what makes you, you. It is your inner thoughts, desires, and motives—the control center of your personhood. There is something deep inside us that is broken because of sin. Since there is something broken inwardly, we do sinful actions outwardly.

Adam and Eve were given a command from God. When they took the fruit and ate it, that was wrong. But the question you have to ask yourself is this: "Why did they do it?" You may answer, "Because Satan tempted them." Yes. But why was it tempting in the first place? A temptation is only tempting if you actually want what is being offered.

> *Sin is a failure to honor God in thought, word, deed, or motive.*

The temptation wasn't just the fruit. It was deeper. It was almost like Satan was asking, "Can you really trust God?" There was something down deep that caused them to doubt that. Something down deep in their hearts didn't believe that God was good or for them. Maybe they just wondered why He would say no to one tree. Maybe they believed there was something God was withholding from them. Maybe they thought God really wasn't for their joy or fulfillment. Maybe they thought there was something more and that eating the fruit would help them see what God was keeping from them.

I am not sure about their exact heart motivation, but at some level, their behavior was saying, "I know God says this, but I want to do this anyway." That is the essence of pride.

Sin always flows from the heart. Our sin is rooted in

unbelief and pride. We don't fully trust God in our depths; therefore we do sinful actions. Maybe the tree illustration will help.

FRUITS

SINFUL BEHAVIORS
lying, stealing, murder,
sexual sin, etc.

SINFUL EFFECTS
shame, guilt,
condemnation, etc.

ROOTS
PRIDE
IDOLATRY
UNBELIEF

What we tend to consider when we think about sin is almost always the fruits of our sinfulness. These are the things we see in ourselves and others. They are the way we feel and the effects of our sinfulness in our minds, attitudes, and emotions.

What the Bible teaches is that sin starts deeper than the fruits. Sin starts in our hearts and then flows to outward behaviors and effects.

This is what Jesus says repeatedly in the Gospels. "What comes out of a person is what defiles them. For it is from within, out of a person's heart, that evil thoughts come—sexual immorality, theft, murder, adultery, greed, malice, deceit, lewdness, envy, slander, arrogance, and folly. All these evils come from inside and defile a person" (Mark 7:20–23).

What is the issue in our hearts? It is the same issue we see in Adam and Eve. We do not fully trust God. We think He may be withholding something good from us. We are tempted to believe that there is something better outside of God and His design.

Sin always flows from the heart.

God should have the primary place in our lives. After all, we were created for this in Genesis 1 and 2. Pride replaces God from the throne of our hearts and places something else there, usually ourselves. This is the essence of idolatry. We should worship God, but we worship something else instead. All this is rooted in unbelief. We don't fully trust God.

When we fail to fully trust God in our hearts, we do sinful actions and reap the sinful effects. Because my heart doesn't fully trust Jesus, I will lie to attempt to get ahead. Because I don't really trust God's plan or design, I don't follow His plan for sexual intimacy. The effects or results of this lack of trust tend to be shame, guilt, and regret. Because I don't find my deepest joy in God, I take my life into my own hands by gossiping, cheating, and deceiving in an attempt to gain and achieve what I think God is withholding from me.

We could give millions of hypothetical examples, but the truth remains. There is something broken in us, so we don't trust God. Because we don't trust God, the result is all kinds of sinful fruit in our lives.

Sin is first and foremost a heart condition. God does not have the primary place in our hearts. That always leads to brokenness. Our sin flows from the depths of our hearts into our attitudes, actions, and beliefs. That is exactly what the Bible and Jesus teach.

> *When we fail to fully trust God in our hearts, we do sinful actions and reap the sinful effects.*

The Result of the Fall

Back to the story. Adam and Eve ate. Their eyes were opened. And it led to death. Death here was not physical death, at least not yet. It would eventually be physical. Immediately, it led to a death of their connectedness to God. To know God is the essence of life. Because of sin, their relationship with God was no longer what it was because sin always separates us from God.

God is always leading us to life. Following His rules and commands always leads to life because

> *The Bible should have been three chapters long.*

it leads us closer to His heart. To disobey God always leads to death because it always leads us away from God's heart and His design for humanity.

At this point in the story and since sin entered the world, all that God created good is fractured and marred. It still functions, but the fullness of all that God created is missed because sin has infected everything.

The Bible should have been three chapters long. With sin now in the world, there is evil, disease, famine, and murder. There is betrayal, sexual immorality, and gossip. I am also convinced that sin is why there are goat head stickers and mosquitoes.

God, who is just, will rightly and properly judge all sin. He could have killed Adam and Eve in the Garden of Eden. He could have destroyed His creation and started over. He would have had every right to do that because Adam and Eve were guilty. That would have been exactly what they deserved. The good news of the gospel is that though we are sinful, God does not leave us in our sin. Rather, in a perfect display of love, God pursues sinful humanity.

This is what the Bible is about and why it doesn't stop after three chapters.

SMALL GROUP QUESTIONS

1. Have you ever learned that the Bible is actually one big story? How does that change how you view it and understand it?

2. What do you think it would have been like to walk with God in the Garden of Eden? Use as many descriptive and sensory words as you can imagine.

3. Before reading this chapter, how did you define sin? How does this chapter give depth and significance to the magnitude of our sin problem?

4. Think of any sin you struggle with. Why do you think you struggle with that specific issue? When you begin asking why, it helps remove the layers biblically to get to the depths of your heart.

5. What does the phrase "the Bible should have been three chapters long" mean? What does that show us about God?

Chapter 4

WHAT IS THE BIBLE ABOUT?

Metanarrative Part 2:
The Beginning

There is tension at this point in God's big story. God made the world good. His heart is for us to know Him and walk with Him in the deepest possible ways. Sin has broken and interrupted our relationship with God, so we are separated from Him.

Instead of throwing it all away, God begins His rescue plan. That leads us to ask these three major questions:

1. How is God going to fix the problem (the curse of sin)?

2. How can sinful people come back into the presence of a holy, sinless God as He designed?

3. If the world is broken, what hope do we have?

God answers these three questions throughout the course of His Bible. I'll summarize the contents of the Bible and attempt to answer these questions.

If we are going to understand the story of the Bible, we will have to spend significant time in Genesis. That is why this chapter is only about the first book of the Bible. There may be moments when you feel like you are getting bogged down, but trust me. I will bring it all together and show you how everything I say relates to the three questions above. Are you ready? You'd better hang on.

First Gospel

Redemption is God bringing mankind back into right relationship with Him. That is at the heart of the story of the Bible. The hero of our redemption is not us. Remember, God is the main character of the Bible, and Jesus is the hero. We cannot save ourselves. We cannot fix our sin problem. We cannot be a good enough person to deserve God's love or forgiveness. We need someone to save us.

> *Redemption is God bringing mankind back into right relationship with Him.*

Think about it like this. On account of our sin, we are rebels committing treason against a Holy God. Biblically, what our sin deserves is an eternity separated from God. That is the definition of hell, and it is awful.

Because God is perfectly just and righteous, He cannot

tolerate our sin and rebellion. We deserve His wrath. We deserve to be punished for our treason. We are guilty. There is no question about it.

You have two options. You can pay for your own sins. Again, this is called hell, an eternal separation from God. Option two is that someone else can pay for your sins.

If you do not understand the depth of your sin, the gospel will never impact you the way it should. To the degree you understand your sinfulness is the same degree that you will see the magnificence of the gospel of Jesus.

I have harped on sin heavily. That being said, sin is never our main focus. It is vital to understand it, but God never leaves us there. Thankfully, God has a plan for all our sins and more. The first glimpse is found in the same chapter that sin is first seen—Genesis 3.

> *If you do not understand the depth of your sin, the gospel will never impact you the way it should.*

So the Lord God said to the serpent, "Because you have done this, cursed are you above all livestock and all wild animals! You will crawl on your belly and you will eat dust all the days of your life. And I will put enmity between you and the woman, and between your offspring and hers; he will crush your head, and you will strike his heel."

—Gen. 3:14–15

Adam and Eve have sinned. It has all been revealed and exposed. God begins cursing Adam, Eve, and the serpent. These verses are so important because God is basically saying that everything is now

> *Genesis 3:14–15 is called the protoevangelium, or the first gospel.*

cursed. But there will come a day when someone who has descended from Adam and Eve will not just wound Satan but will crush him. There is a descendent from Adam and Eve who will have a definitive victory.

Genesis 3:14–15 is called the protoevangelium, or the first gospel. It is the first indication or foreshadowing of the great rescue plan God will pull off through Jesus Christ. This is the story of the Bible. It is the story of redemption.

Redemption - Genesis 3 Through Revelation 20

This begins the third of four sections of our big overview (Creation, Fall, Redemption, Restoration). Obviously, I can't tell every part of the story and must either skip or summarize some parts. My goal is to hit the highlights so you can trace the activity of God all the way through Jesus to us today. We will see many themes reiterated throughout the story. There are parallels, hints, and shadows. We will take some turns that seem like detours that really make the story much deeper and more beautiful.

Are you ready?

After Adam and Eve sin, God curses them and the serpent.

God then kills an animal and makes clothing for Adam and Eve (Gen. 3:21).

That brings us to a theme that we will see repeatedly—something innocent dying for the guilty. Remember this! After God banishes Adam and Eve from the Garden of Eden, they begin populating the world.

> *Recurring theme: something innocent dying for the guilty.*

Sin did not just enter the world in Genesis 3. Biblically, since Adam and Eve sinned, sin now passed down to all mankind. All people are born into sin. Everyone needs a savior.

Adam and Eve have sons named Cain and Abel (Gen. 4). Abel works with the flocks and herds of animals. Cain tends the ground. They both bring their firstfruits to offer to God. For some reason, God accepts Abel's sacrifice but doesn't accept Cain's. We can speculate, but I think it has to do with their hearts. "By faith Abel brought God a better offering than Cain did" (Heb. 11:4). The result is that Cain is furious, and the next time they are in the field, Cain murders Abel.

> *The Lord said, "What have you done? Listen! Your brother's blood cries out to me from the ground. Now you are under a curse and driven from the ground, which opened its mouth to receive your brother's blood from your hand. When you work the ground, it will no longer yield its crops for you. You will be a restless wanderer on the earth."*
>
> —Gen. 4:10–12

Cain is banished to become a wanderer.

Adam and Eve have another son, Seth. This is important. We must remember that Genesis 3 says the one who will crush Satan will descend from Adam and Eve. He can't go through Abel who is killed and does not seem to have had any children. The promise of Genesis 3:15 will not go through Cain. It will go through Seth.

As the story continues, Genesis 5 gives us the genealogy that leads to Noah. It just so happens that Noah is a descendent of Seth (Gen. 5:6, 29).

You have probably heard the story of Noah. Everyone is sinful and wicked, so God decides to destroy the earth, but He chooses to preserve Noah and his family. There are eight people who will be saved.

Noah faithfully builds the ark. God sends the animals (Gen. 7:9). At the appointed time, God shuts the ark's door. Rain falls from the heavens, and at the same time, water crashes up from the ground (Gen. 7:11–12). There is a massive flood that kills all the people in the world except for Noah and his family. They are safe only because they have taken refuge in the ark as God directed.

Once the flood is over, God reiterates the mandate with Noah that He had given to Adam and Eve—to be fruitful and multiply (Gen. 1:28, 9:7). Noah and his family begin repopulating the earth.

That leads us to the end of Genesis 11 where we are introduced to Abram.

Again, if you are annoyed at the genealogies, just remember

that they play a vital role in helping us fully connect all the dots that God wants us to connect.

Abram is a descendant of Noah who is a descent of Seth, the son of Adam and Eve. Genesis 12 is arguably one of the most important chapters in the Bible.

> *The Lord had said to Abram, "Go from your country, your people and your father's household to the land I will show you. I will make you into a great nation, and I will bless you; I will make your name great, and you will be a blessing. I will bless those who bless you, and whoever curses you I will curse; and all peoples on earth will be blessed through you."*
>
> —Gen. 12:1–3

This is the call of Abram. It is also the beginning of God's covenant with Abram.

God will reiterate and add a little to His promise in Genesis 15. He will do the same thing in Genesis 17 where He will also change Abram's name to Abraham and introduce circumcision. The theme of covenant is extremely important. One of the core questions deals with how a sinful people can come back into the presence of a holy God. Part of that answer has to do with this idea of covenant. A covenant is a divine agreement between God and people. Wayne Grudem in Systematic Theology calls it an "unchangeable, divinely imposed legal agreement between God and man that stipulates the conditions of their relationship."[11]

A contract is different than a covenant. A contract says if you do your part, I'll do my part. If you make a contract with someone to build your house, you pay them money, and they build your house.

> *A covenant is a divine agreement between God and people.*

If you don't pay the money, they won't build your house. If you pay the money, you can expect them to build your house. If they don't, you can legally take them to court because they have not fulfilled their part of the contract. In a contract, both parties do their part.

A covenant is a deep, relational binding. God covenants with Abraham. That means God was committing to Abraham and his descendants. There were stipulations to this covenant. If humanity obeys, there will be blessings (Deut. 28). If they don't obey, there will be curses (there are curses throughout the rest of the Old Testament, but we will get to that in the next chapter). The difference in God's covenant and a contract is that even though we prove to be faithless over and over, God is always faithful to keep His word and fulfill His covenant.

God's faithfulness does not depend on our faithfulness. This is extremely good news for us.

The covenant God makes with Abraham in Genesis 12, 15, and 17 has three major biblical themes—land, seed, and blessing. The theme of land has to do with God giving His people the Promised Land as described in the book of Joshua. For our purposes, I will zero in and focus on the fact that through

Abraham's seed—his offspring or children—the whole world will be blessed.

What I am about to say is super important, so make sure you get it. Abraham's descendants are called the Jewish people, the Hebrews, or the Israelites. If you are not a descendant of Abraham, you are a Gentile. This is another major theme in the Bible.

The big problem with Genesis 12, 15, and 17 is that God is making all these promises about Abraham's descendants, but Abraham doesn't have a son yet. That leads us to the miraculous birth of Abraham's son, Isaac.

> Abraham's descendants are called the Jewish people, the Hebrews, or the Israelites.

God enables Sarah, Abraham's wife, to conceive even though she has been barren. When she gets pregnant, she is 90 years old, and Abraham is 100 (Gen. 17:17, 21:5). Isaac is born, and then we come to Genesis 22.

Understanding the covenant and the promises God gave changes the way we read this chapter.

> *Take your son, your only son, whom you love—Isaac— and go to the region of Moriah. Sacrifice him there as a burnt offering on a mountain I will show you.*
>
> —Gen. 22:2

There are so many problems with this verse. God had made promises about Abraham's descendants, and this verse seems to say that God has changed His mind. Abraham and Sarah are old. This son was already miraculous. Could God give them another son if Isaac dies? And why would God ask Abraham to do this? It is confusing.

But Abraham obeys.

For three days, Abraham, Isaac, and their servants walk to the place God instructed them to go. Abraham knew what God had asked, and he had to be struggling. When they get close, Abraham leaves the servants behind.

He and Isaac begin to walk up the mountain. Isaac literally carries the wood he is supposed to be laid on. They get to the top. Abraham prepares the altar. Then he lays Isaac on the wood. It had to be a crazy moment. Isaac had to be freaking out, right?

As Abraham lifts up his hand to strike his son, the angel of the Lord stops him.

Abraham has passed the test. Isaac doesn't have to die. In fact, there is a ram caught in the brush that Abraham can use as a substitute for Isaac.

Abraham looked up and there in a thicket he saw a ram caught by its horns. He went over and took the ram and sacrificed it as a burnt offering instead of his son. So Abraham called that place The Lord Will Provide. And to this day it is said, "On the mountain of the Lord it will be provided." The angel of the Lord called to Abraham from heaven a second time and said, "I swear by myself, declares the Lord, that because you have done this and have not withheld your son, your only son, I will surely bless you and make your descendants as numerous as the stars in the sky and as the sand on the seashore. Your descendants will take possession of the cities of their enemies, and through your offspring all nations on earth will be blessed, because you have obeyed me."

—Gen. 22:13–18

What recurring themes do we see here? We see an innocent dying as a substitute (verse 13), promised blessings for obedience (verse 16), descendants becoming a nation (verse 17), descendants possessing land (verses 17–18), and the world blessed through Abraham (verse 18).

> *The covenant of God that starts with Abraham is passed down through Isaac.*

Thus, the covenant of God that started with Abraham is passed down through Isaac.

As the story goes, Isaac marries Rebekah, and they have two sons—Jacob and Esau. They are twins, but Esau was born first and is thus the oldest. Both Jacob and Esau seem shady to me. More than once, Jacob tricks Esau. He tricks him out of his birthright (Gen. 25:29–34) and steals Esau's blessing (Gen. 27).

In Genesis 27, Jacob and his mother work together to deceive Isaac to steal Esau's blessing. As Isaac is getting old, he wants to bless his oldest son, Esau. This was customary in their culture.

Rebekah hears Isaac tell Esau to go kill and cook good wild game and then bring it to him, and then he will bless him. Rebekah quickly goes and kills a lamb. They put goat hair on Jacob's arms because Esau is hairy. They put Jacob in Esau's clothes, so he smells like Esau.

When Jacob brings the food in, Isaac is impressed that it all happened so fast.

Because Isaac is blind, he isn't sure who has come in. It sounds like Jacob, but the arms feel like Esau. The clothes smell like Esau.

As the story goes, Isaac gives Jacob the blessing that was supposed to go to Esau. That obviously infuriates Esau. Long story short, Isaac sends Jacob away to find a wife from his descendants. He wants Jacob to marry a descendant of Abraham, not a local Gentile woman.

On the journey one night, Jacob has a dream. He sees a ladder going from earth to the heavens. God and the angels are ascending and descending, and God appears to Jacob.

There above it stood the Lord, and he said: "I am the Lord, the God of your father Abraham and the God of Isaac. I will give you and your descendants the land on which you are lying. Your descendants will be like the dust of the earth, and you will spread out to the west and to the east, to the north and to the south. All peoples on earth will be blessed through you and your offspring. I am with you and will watch over you wherever you go, and I will bring you back to this land. I will not leave you until I have done what I have promised you."

—Gen. 28:13–15

God's covenant has now passed from Abraham to Isaac and now to Jacob.

There is one more story of Jacob that I want to tell you briefly. It is in Genesis 32. Jacob has married Leah and Rachel. He has 11 sons from both of them and from his two female maidservants, Bilhah and Zilpah. He is now on his way back to where he is from, and there is a story where he wrestles with God. It is a very odd story.

One night, Jacob was alone, and a man wrestled him all night. Neither Jacob nor the man overpowered the other. Toward the end of the night, the unnamed man touches Jacob's hip. It pops out of

> *God's covenant has now passed from Abraham to Isaac and now to Jacob.*

its socket, but Jacob does not let go. Jacob says he will not let go unless the man blesses him. Then the man asks what his name is, and he says Jacob.

Then the man says he will no longer be called Jacob, but Israel.

Then the man said, "Let me go, for it is daybreak." But Jacob replied, "I will not let you go unless you bless me." The man asked him, "What is your name?" "Jacob," he answered. Then the man said, "Your name will no longer

*be Jacob, but Israel, because you have struggled with God
and with humans and have overcome."*

—Gen. 32:26–28

I think there is a lot of depth here because Jacob's first blessing was a stolen blessing from his brother. This one is different.

It is also significant because Jacob receives his new name,
Israel. He currently has 11 sons. In Genesis 35, Rachel has
one last son named Benjamin, but she dies as she is giving
birth. That gives Jacob 12 sons. The 12 sons of Jacob, or Israel,
become the 12 tribes of Israel.

Judah and Joseph

As we are tracing the promises of God flowing through the
generations, we now have to ask who it will flow to next. The
end of Genesis includes almost 10 chapters about Joseph. This
is a famous story that deserves way more than I am about to
say.

Here is a summary. Joseph's brothers sell him into slavery. He ends up in Egypt, is falsely accused, and ends up in
prison. Through a series of crazy God-ordained events, Joseph
ends up being the second in command in Egypt. He becomes
instrumental in saving the world from a worldwide famine. In
the end, he is reunited with his brothers and forgives them.
By the end of the book of Geneses, the whole family ends up
in Egypt.

Are you ready to nerd out? Most people read Joseph and

learn tons of lessons, but they miss some of the deeper meaning behind the story. One of the primary reasons the story of Joseph is told has nothing to do with Joseph at all. It has to do with how God's promise from Genesis 12 will pass to the next generation.

In Jewish culture, the firstborn son inherits the most. The blessings pass to him. That is one reason that Jacob's stealing his older brother's birthright and blessing was so culturally off. He was younger. It was culturally inappropriate.

The assumption was that Jacob's oldest son would receive the blessing. If not him, then the next, and so on. Humanly speaking, the promises of God should go from Abraham to Isaac to Jacob and then to Reuben, the firstborn of Jacob. If not to Reuben then to Simeon the secondborn. If not to Simeon, then to Levi the thirdborn. But it does not go to any of these brothers.

Let me show you some things. If you aren't looking for them or if you have never been shown, they almost seem odd and out of place as you read through the book of Genesis. I am fascinated by these details because, at the surface level, they seem like random inserted facts that don't help the narrative. There are moments where the Bible is talking about Jacob, and then it seems to stop and talk about Dinah in Genesis 34 and then go back to Jacob.

It happens again in the story of Joseph, whose story begins in Genesis 37. Then in Genesis 38, it stops talking about Joseph and talks about Judah and Tamar. Then Genesis 39 goes back to Joseph.

Why is the Bible interrupting itself in Genesis 34 and 38? I am glad you asked.

In Genesis 34, Dinah, one of Jacob's daughters, is raped by a local ruler, a pagan Gentile who was a Hivite. Even though he defiles her, this guy loves Dinah and wants his father to get her so he can marry her.

Jacob hears about Dinah being defiled and does nothing about it (a whole other story). When Dinah's brothers Simeon and Levi hear the news, they are furious. How could they let this defilement stand?

The guy who raped Dinah offers to marry her for any bride price. This group of people offers to intermarry with the Jewish people and mix themselves in, which God had forbidden.

Simeon and Levi respond deceitfully. They "agree" to the offer for Dinah on one condition. They ask that all males in that specific local people group get circumcised. The Hivite people agree! Now that's love.

Here's what happens.

Three days later, while all of them were still in pain, two of Jacob's sons, Simeon and Levi, Dinah's brothers, took their swords and attacked the unsuspecting city, killing every male.

—Gen. 34:25

Simeon and Levi are Jacob's second and third sons. They are the ones who kill this clan of people. Tuck that away and remember it.

In Genesis 35, we see Reuben, the firstborn. Watch how these details are thrown in here.

So Rachel died and was buried on the way to Ephrath (that is, Bethlehem). Over her tomb Jacob set up a pillar, and to this day that pillar marks Rachel's tomb. Israel moved on again and pitched his tent beyond Migdal Eder. While Israel was living in that region, Reuben went in and slept with his father's concubine Bilhah, and Israel heard of it. Jacob had twelve sons: The sons of Leah: Reuben the firstborn of Jacob, Simeon, Levi, Judah, Issachar and Zebulun. The sons of Rachel: Joseph and Benjamin. The sons of Rachel's servant Bilhah: Dan and Naphtali. The sons of Leah's servant Zilpah: Gad and Asher. These were the sons of Jacob, who were born to him in Paddan Aram.

—Gen. 35:19–26

Are you following? Did you see that seemingly random verse that tells us Reuben did something forbidden? Hold on. I will make it make sense.

We see Simeon and Levi get wild in Genesis 34. We see Reuben make a terrible mistake in Genesis 35. The story of Joseph starts in Genesis 37 and then interrupts itself in Genesis 38 to tell us about Judah and Tamar. Judah is the fourthborn son of Jacob. Genesis 39 picks up where Genesis 37 leaves off in the story of Joseph. Genesis 38 is weird if you don't understand it.

Here is the story of Genesis 38. Judah has two sons, Er and Onan. Judah gets Er a wife named Tamar. Er is wicked, so God puts him to death. In Hebrew culture, if your brother's wife dies without a son, you are to do your part to get her pregnant, raise a son, and carry on your brother's line. This is the idea of the Kinsman Redeemer that comes up in the book of Ruth as well. (There is also a story where they give Jesus this kind of cultural riddle that involved the Kinsman Redeemer in Mark 12:18–27.)

After Er dies, it's the brother Onan's job to help carry on his brother's line.

> *Then Judah said to Onan, "Sleep with your brother's wife and fulfill your duty to her as a brother-in-law to raise up offspring for your brother." But Onan knew that the child would not be his; so whenever he slept with his brother's wife, he spilled his semen on the ground to keep from providing offspring for his brother. What he did was wicked in the Lord's sight; so the Lord put him to death also.*
>
> —Gen. 38:8–10

Onan fails to do what he is called to do in that culture, and it is wicked. The dad, Judah, has a plan. Judah makes an agreement with Tamar to live as a widow until his youngest son, Shelah, grows up. Once he becomes of age, it will be his responsibility to give her an heir.

In the course of time, Judah's wife dies, and Judah goes back to the area where Tamar is living. Tamar hears about that and spies on them. She realizes that Shelah is of age, but Judah has not kept his promise.

She devises a plan. When I used to read this story, I thought she was shady. In reality, it is Judah who is shady because he has not kept his word. Tamar dresses as a prostitute, covers her face, and goes into Judah, who says he will pay her by sending her a goat later. She asks for collateral or a pledge, and he gives her his personal seal and cord. When she gets the goat, she will return the collateral.

Judah sleeps with her and gets her pregnant, but he doesn't know it. When he comes back to pay, Tamar is nowhere to be found, and no one knows what Judah is talking about because there isn't a prostitute who typically hangs out there.

Once Tamar begins to show that she is pregnant, Judah finds out and thinks she has been unfaithful. He confronts her, and she shows him his own cord and seal that he had left for collateral. Judah admits that she acted righteously and that he acted wickedly (Gen. 38:26). Judah should have provided his youngest son to carry on his other son's name.

That story seems odd until you finish reading the book. In Genesis 39–50, we are back to Joseph.

As the story goes, when Joseph is in power in Egypt and the famine is hurting the entire world, Joseph's brothers come to him for grain. They assume Joseph is gone or dead. They could have never imagined or predicted that the brother they sold into slavery is the second in command in the greatest superpower in the world.

When they come to Joseph, he inquires about his full

brother, Benjamin, and his father, Jacob. The 10 brothers don't realize what Joseph is doing.

Joseph tells them he thinks they are spies and says that unless they bring Benjamin to him, they will never get grain. He puts Simeon in prison until they return.

When the nine brothers go back to Jacob, they tell him everything, and he's furious. But nothing happens until they run out of grain again.

They have to convince Jacob to let Benjamin go with them or they know they won't be able to buy any grain. We don't have time to read all the accounts, but you can read Genesis 43:8–14 to see how Judah takes responsibility for the safety of Benjamin.

Then as you continue reading into Genesis 44, Joseph tricks them again and basically makes it look like Benjamin stole from him. As they go back to confront Joseph, they think Benjamin and maybe all of them are about to die. There is a long conversation between Judah and Joseph. Here is how it ends.

> *"Your servant my father said to us, 'You know that my wife bore me two sons. One of them went away from me, and I said, "He has surely been torn to pieces." And I have not seen him since. If you take this one from me too and harm comes to him, you will bring my gray head down to the grave in misery.' "So now, if the boy is not with us when I go back to your servant my father, and if my father, whose life is closely bound up with the boy's life, sees that the boy isn't there, he will die. Your servants will*

bring the gray head of our father down to the grave in sorrow. Your servant guaranteed the boy's safety to my father. I said, 'If I do not bring him back to you, I will bear the blame before you, my father, all my life!' Now then, please let your servant remain here as my lord's slave in place of the boy, and let the boy return with his brothers. How can I go back to my father if the boy is not with me? No! Do not let me see the misery that would come on my father."

—Gen. 44:27–34

Judah takes responsibility for Benjamin. That is huge because before the brothers sold Joseph into slavery, Judah was leading the way in that (Gen. 37:26–27). But in Genesis 44, Judah is literally substituting himself for Benjamin. I think that plays into what we see in Genesis 49.

> *In Genesis 44, Judah is substituting himself for Benjamin.*

By this time in the story, all the Jewish people—Jacob, his wives, all his sons and their wives, all his grandkids—have moved to Egypt to survive and escape the famine. All the descendants of Abraham are in Egypt. Joseph has saved the world as second in command to Pharaoh.

Jacob is getting old and about to die. He calls his 12 sons in to bless them.

Then Jacob called for his sons and said: "Gather around so I can tell you what will happen to you in days to come.

Assemble and listen, sons of Jacob; listen to your father Israel. Reuben, you are my firstborn, my might, the first sign of my strength, excelling in honor, excelling in power. Turbulent as the waters, you will no longer excel, for you went up onto your father's bed, onto my couch and defiled it. Simeon and Levi are brothers— their swords are weapons of violence. Let me not enter their council, let me not join their assembly, for they have killed men in their anger and hamstrung oxen as they pleased. Cursed be their anger, so fierce, and their fury, so cruel! I will scatter them in Jacob and disperse them in Israel. Judah, your brothers will praise you; your hand will be on the neck of your enemies; your father's sons will bow down to you. You are a lion's cub, Judah; you return from the prey, my son. Like a lion he crouches and lies down, like a lioness—who dares to rouse him? The scepter will not depart from Judah, nor the ruler's staff from between his feet, until he to whom it belongs shall come and the obedience of the nations shall be his. He will tether his donkey to a vine, his colt to the choicest branch; he will wash his garments in wine, his robes in the blood of grapes. His eyes will be darker than wine, his teeth whiter than milk.

—Gen. 49:1–12

God promised Abraham so much in Genesis 12, 15, and 17. That promise passed to his son Isaac and from Isaac to Jacob, also known as Israel. Now it has passed through Judah.

Through Judah's lineage, we will eventually see how the whole world will be blessed.

Even though Judah does seem to have a better character development than Reuben, Simeon, or Levi, he still was not worthy of the covenant to pass through him. Actually, no one is worthy. We see grace here that foreshadows the gospel so many centuries later. God is a God who gives us not what we deserve but what we don't deserve by His incredible, unexplainable grace. That is the definition of grace—getting what you do not deserve. Be mindful as you continue reading to see how God consistently gives His people grace.

At the close of Genesis, God's people do not have any land that God has promised, but that will come later. They currently consist of around 70 people (Gen. 46:26–

> *Grace is getting what you do not deserve.*

27). By the time the second book of the Bible begins, much has changed.

I am aware that this chapter probably felt like too much information. But if we don't understand the beginnings, the rest will not make sense. If you don't understand Genesis, the story will have massive missing pieces. It will be like watching a movie but starting halfway through it. We must understand God's heart in creation. We must feel the weight of sin and the fall. As Genesis plays out, we must see God faithfully walking with His people to fulfill and accomplish all His promises.

In the next chapter, we will be speeding up, and I pray it will be as fascinating to you as it is to me.

── SMALL GROUP QUESTIONS ──

1. Define redemption (see the section "First Gospel"). What happened that broke our relationship with God?

2. In your own words, describe the importance of Genesis 3:14–15 and Genesis 12:1–3.

3. How is a covenant different than a contract? What does that teach us about God?

4. List all the names the Bible uses to refer to the descendants of Abraham.

5. Summarize the message of Genesis in your own words. (If you don't understand the beginning, the story will be much harder to follow as we go.)

Chapter 5

WHAT IS THE BIBLE ABOUT?

Metanarrative Part 3:
The Old Testament

We had to get through Genesis, so the rest of the story makes sense. Now we are about to speed up. Do you remember our core questions we must attempt to answer in light of Genesis 1–3?

1. How is God going to fix the problem (the curse of sin)?

2. How can sinful people come back into the presence of a holy, sinless God?

3. If the world is broken, what hope do we have?

Exiting Egypt

The book of Genesis ends with all of God's people (the descendants of Abraham, Jews, Israelites, Hebrews—all words for the same group of people) living in Egypt (Exod. 1:5). When we come to Exodus, the main point of the book is different than Genesis, which laid a foundation and helps us see what God's covenant was and how it passed from generation to generation. Exodus will address the issue of how we approach God. How can a sinful people come into the presence of a holy and just God without dying?

From the end of Genesis to the beginning of Exodus, 430 years have passed. In that time (Exod. 12:40), the Egyptians have taken the Israelites captive as slaves and forced them into manual, hard labor every day all year round (Exod. 1:11). They have no days off, no hope of a future, and no hope that their lives will ever be anything else. They begin to cry out to God, and He listens. God's answer comes with the birth of Moses.

Moses was supposed to be killed by order of the Pharaoh that all Israelite boys were to be killed upon birth (Exod. 1:16). The 70 people at the end of Genesis has now become over a million as estimated by some scholars. The killing of Israelite boys was the Egyptians' attempt to limit the growth of the Israelites.

In Exodus 2, Moses is put into a basket in the Nile to preserve his life. Pharaoh's daughter sees him and takes him into her home. Moses is raised for 40 years with the best food, best education, and most luxurious lifestyle possible at that time.

When he is 40, he sees an Egyptian taskmaster beat an Israelite, and he steps in but ends up killing the Egyptian. He hides the body and assumes he is clear.

The next day, he sees two Israelites fighting and breaks it up. They respond by asking if he is going to kill them like he did the Egyptian the day before. Moses gets scared and flees.

Moses spends the next 40 years in Midian where he tends sheep. He gets married and has children. He is doing perfectly fine until one day he sees a bush burning in the distance. The problem is that the bush isn't being consumed. It just keeps burning (Exod. 3–4).

As Moses approaches the bush, God speaks. Long story short, God calls Moses to return to Egypt and demand Pharaoh to let his people go. God tells Moses to then lead God's people—the Jewish people, the descendants of Abraham—to the land God has promised them.

Long story short (again), Moses goes back and demands Pharaoh to let his people go. Pharaoh refuses, and the 10 plagues ensue. Those 10 plagues are fascinating and show God's complete power and control over not just nature but over kings and kingdoms, everything the Egyptians hold dear. The 10th plague is the death of the firstborn (Exod. 11–12). This is extremely important to the big story.

It is the night the first Passover meal happens. The meal will be repeated every year as a Jewish holiday to celebrate and remember what God was about to do. It is the same meal Jesus and His disciples ate the night before His death (the Last Supper).

Back in Egypt, the main idea is that each Hebrew family will slaughter a lamb and eat it. The first night (Exod. 11–12), they are

> *Innocent blood covers the guilty.*

to take blood from that lamb and smear it on their doorposts, which will protect them from the death angel who will kill the firstborn of every family whose house is not covered by the blood of the lamb. If the blood of the innocent, spotless lamb is on the doorframe of a house, the death angel will "pass over" that house.

Do you remember one of our recurring themes? Innocent blood covers the guilty. This theme goes back to Adam and Eve in Genesis 3 where the innocent animal died to cover Adam and Eve. In Exodus, an innocent lamb will die to save the firstborn of every household.

On Passover night, all the firstborn in Egypt die, except those households that are covered by the blood. The Egyptians send the Israelites out in a frenzy. What is wild is that the Egyptians give the Israelites all kinds of gold and expensive jewelry. The Bible says the Israelites plunder the Egyptians on the way out (Exod. 12:35–36). It seems like an awkward detail, but it will come back into play when we get to the Tabernacle.

The firstborn in Egypt die. The Israelites go in haste. God leads them by fire at night and by a cloud during the day (Exod. 13:21–22). Can you imagine this? The teacher in me is cringing at all the details I have to brush over. God has shown His miraculous power in the 10 plagues. He has manifested His presence in a cloud by day and the pillar of fire by night. He is literally leading the people with Moses at the head. Moses leads them all the way to the Red Sea.

The Pharaoh and the Egyptians decide they made a bad choice and want their slaves back. So they begin to pursue them (Exod. 14:5).

Imagine holding everything you own. All your family is present. All your animals, cookware, clothes, possessions, and everything are there. You are facing a massive sea with no boat. You have mountains on one side and a desert on the other. You can't go back because the massive Egyptian army is in hot pursuit. This scene must have been intense.

What does God do? He does what only God can do. He moves behind the Israelites and puts Himself between the Egyptians and His people (Exod. 14:19). Then God parts the Red Sea so the Israelites can walk through the sea on dry ground (Exod. 14:21–22, 29).

I have always wondered how this looked. Was it like an aquarium but with no glass? Were the people freaking out that the ground was dry?

Were there little kids trying to see the fish, but their parents were shooing them along? It is an awesome thought to try to put yourself into the story to see and feel it.

Once the Israelites are safely across and the Egyptians are attempting to follow, the ground becomes muddy, and the Egyptians get stuck. Then the waters crash back down, and the Egyptian army all drown (Exod. 14:23–28). God gets yet another victory over the Egyptian people.

God's people have been delivered from their slavery in Egypt and are now headed to the Promised Land (modern-day Middle East). It is the land God promised Abraham in Genesis 12, hundreds of years before this moment.

So much is going to happen in the wilderness on the way to the Promised Land. God's people will grumble and complain a lot. Three days after the Exodus, they are complaining about food and water, which I used to make fun of. The more I think about it, the more I realize it does make sense for them to complain. They had families, little kids, and animals. You have to have food and water. If you didn't have food and water for three days, it wouldn't matter what God had done five days ago. You would be in a terrible state both physically and spiritually.

Even though it makes human sense that God's people are upset, what we begin to see is that even from the beginning, God's people lack in trusting Him. There is a lack of faith in His promises. This is another recurring theme.

At this point in the story, God is still moving the people by a cloud in the day and by fire at night. When God stops, they stop. When God moves, they move.

For food, God provides manna and quail (Exod. 16). Every day, the Israelites wake up and gather food for the day. If they gather extra, it spoils. They gather only what they need for the day. On the sixth day, Friday, they gather double, and it

> *The core of our sin issue is a lack of trust in God, which leads us to live in unbelief.*

doesn't spoil. They do that so they can rest and not gather on the Sabbath, the seventh day, Saturday.

As this massive group of people move toward the Promised Land, more than once they are in a spot where they need water (Exod. 17). They complain to Moses, and Moses complains to God, who tells Moses to strike the rock. Moses strikes the rock, and water flows out for all the people.

Here again we see the theme of lack of trust in God. The people don't really trust God as He attempts to lead them. They struggle when things don't go their way. They rebel against Moses. They doubt God.

Before we are too critical, know that this is the core of our sin issue. We don't trust God, and it leads us to live in unbelief. The Israelites don't trust God. They don't think God will provide, so they grumble and complain. We literally do the same thing. Learn from the Israelites, but don't be too hard on them. If we were in their spot, I think we might have acted exactly the same way.

In Numbers 13 and 14, Moses has led the people all the way to the Promised Land. Remember, this is the land God promised to give His people in Genesis 12. They send in 12 spies to check out the land. They come back and say the land is just like God promised—it is incredible. They do say there is a "small" problem—the giants. The cities are also highly fortified. Ten of the 12 spies give a negative report. Joshua and Caleb are ready to go, but the other 10 are scared.

As a result of their lack of faith, God makes the people wander in the wilderness for 40 years until that generation dies off. During this wilderness wandering, God leads Moses to the top of Mount Sinai and gives him the Old Testament Law. In that Law are things like the Ten Commandments, the instructions for the Tabernacle, and more.

Law and Tabernacle

The Law can have a very negative connotation today, but the Law was good. It did three overarching things for God's people.

- It guided them as a nation.

- It guided them relationally with one another.

- It instructed them on how to approach the living God.

For our purposes, we want to zero in on how to approach God because that is one of our overarching questions—how does a sinful people approach a holy and just God?

We have established that sin entered the world in Genesis 3. Now we have all sinned and fall short of God's glory. We want to come back into God's presence like we were designed, but we can't because we are sinful. And if God is just, He must deal with our sin. He can't brush it under the rug, or He wouldn't be a just judge. He can't pretend it isn't there because that would be lying. How can God love us and still punish sin? How can God deal with sin and not kill us? God's Law and the sacrificial system show us.

The Law shows us how sinful we are. It shows us God's

righteous standard. As it turns out, no one could keep it fully, properly, or perfectly with their heart and actions always in line. The Law didn't just show God's people their

> *If God is just, He must deal with our sin.*

sinfulness; it also showed them what to do after they sinned—namely, sacrifice something innocent to stand in place of the guilty.

The Law also established the Tabernacle or the Temple. The Tabernacle was a portable tent where God's presence rested among the camp of the Israelites. Eventually, Solomon would build a permanent Temple when God's people were settled in the Promised Land and no longer wandering (1 Kings 6). The Tabernacle had three sections: the outer court, the inner court, and the Holy of Holies.

Think about this. How did Israelite slaves who escaped Egypt and were walking in the desert get materials to build a portable Tabernacle? Much of the Tabernacle had to be overlayed with gold. It was a magnificent structure. Remember earlier in our story when the Israelites left Egypt? The Bible says they plundered the Egyptians and took all kinds of gold and jewelry (Exod. 12:36). The people then gave the gold and other precious items as an offering so God's Tabernacle could be built, and all the garments and curtains could be made. Fascinating!

Back to the Tabernacle structure. All of God's people were allowed in the outer court where they brought their sacrifices and made their offerings on the bronze altar. The bronze laver held water, which was used for various washings. The priests and the people had daily offerings and duties, a host of things prescribed by God.

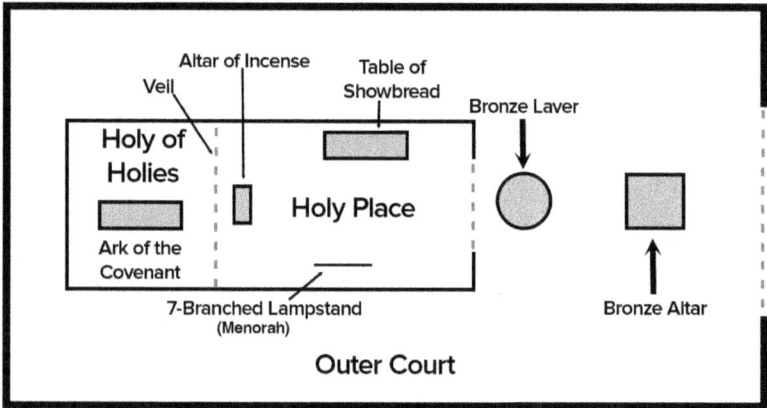

While everyone could enter the outer court, only the priests ministering on duty could enter the inner court, or the Holy Place. They had various practices and duties there that God prescribed. There were candles that had to be tended to on the menorah or lampstand. The Table of Showbread required bread to continually be tended to and replaced. Incense had to be burned on the Altar of Incense.

Beyond the inner court was a huge veil that blocked the entrance to the Holy of Holies. Inside the Holy of Holies was the Ark of the Covenant, a rectangular box. On top of this ark were two cherubim (heavenly like creatures). Between the two cherubim and on top of the ark was where the actual presence of God rested (Exod. 25).

The Holy of Holies was only accessible by the High Priest one day per year—the Day of Atonement (Lev. 16). Atonement has to do with paying a penalty. Remember, our sin makes us guilty. Atonement is what is paid to cover that guilt. A recurring theme is that something innocent must die to cover the guilty. That is the idea of atonement.

> *The Holy of Holies was only accessible by the High Priest one day per year—the Day of Atonement.*

There is a lot of detail about what the High Priest had to do on the Day of Atonement. He had to bathe multiple times. There were rules about his clothing. It was an extremely important and detailed day.

On that day, the High Priest sacrificed an innocent lamb for himself to make atonement for him and his household. He had to take that blood into the Holy of Holies and sprinkle it over the Ark of the Covenant.

Then he took two goats, presented them before the Lord in the entrance of the Tabernacle, and cast lots over them. One lot was for the Lord, and one was for the scapegoat. The High Priest took the one the lot fell on and sacrificed it to the Lord as a sin offering. He slaughtered the goat in front of the people. Then he took it into the Holy of Holies and sprinkled the blood over the Ark of the Covenant. When he came out, he laid his hands over the goat chosen as the scapegoat and confessed all the sins of the Israelites. After that, he sent the goat away into the wilderness, symbolizing the carrying away of their sins.

The High Priest was the mediator between God's people and God. He only passed the veil of the Holy of Holies one day per year on the Day of Atonement (Heb. 9:7). On that day, he sacrifices for himself and then on behalf of the people. He did this year after year to make atonement for sins. An innocent lamb or goat died in place of the guilty, and the blood covered the Israelites' sins for another year. The High Priest confessed the sins of the people over the scapegoat that carried their sins away.

What do we learn from all this? It seems so barbaric. It is so bloody and brutal. One thing we learn is that no one measures up to God's righteous standard. We all sin and fall short. No one can perfectly keep the Law. But God, in His grace and mercy, made a way for God's people to approach Him. He makes a way for sin to be dealt with.

God makes a way for us to be able to worship Him. Do you see the heart of God even in the Law and the sacrificial system? It is a really deep and beautiful thing.

> *No one measures up to God's righteous standard. We all sin and fall short.*

Blessings and Curses

Before Moses dies, he gives a lot of instruction to the people. Some of those instructions are found in Deuteronomy 28. Moses explains that if God's people follow God, His abundant blessings will flow. But it depends on how God's people respond. Are they going to live for God, or are they going to follow idols? If they don't follow God, curses are going to come.

If you fully obey the Lord your God and carefully follow all his commands I give you today, the Lord your God will set you high above all the nations on earth. All these blessings will come on you and accompany you if you obey the Lord your God.

—Deut. 28:1–2

Then the Bible goes on to list many blessings:

1. In the city and in the country

2. Fruit of your womb

3. Crops of your land

4. Young of your livestock

5. Basket and kneading trough

6. Blessing against enemies

7. Barns and all you put in your hands

8. Establish you as His holy people

9. Open the heavens, send rain, and bless all the work of your hands

Sounds pretty good, right? These are the things we ask for all the time, and God says He will give them to His people if they obey Him. But if they don't . . . curses.

*However, if you do not obey the Lord your God and do not
carefully follow all his commands and decrees I am giving
you today, all these curses will come on you and overtake
you.*

—Deut. 28:15

Curses. Everything He said He would bless, He will now
curse. And ultimately, they would be defeated by their enemies.

*The Lord will drive you and the king you set over you to
a nation unknown to you or your ancestors. There you
will worship other gods, gods of wood and stone. You will
become a thing of horror, a byword and an object of ridi-
cule among all the peoples where the Lord will drive you.*

—Deut. 28:36–37

Let me generalize Joshua through Malachi, or the rest of
the Old Testament. There will be a few really good times where
God's people follow Him and He
blesses them like crazy. But then
they will walk away from God, and
literally everything God promises in
Deuteronomy 28 will come true. A
few hundred years after Moses dies,
God's people will be taken captive
just like God said would happen.

> *The summary of
> the Old Testament
> is God's people
> consistently
> walking away
> from God.*

In fact, when you read through the rest of the Old Testament,
especially 1 and 2 Kings and 1 and 2 Chronicles and almost all

the prophets, you should keep Deuteronomy 28 marked and reference it often.

Let's go back to our story with the death of Moses.

Joshua and Judges

When Moses died, he had led the Israelites in the wilderness for 40 years. He led them to the edge of the Promised Land, but he didn't get to enter. Joshua has now taken over for Moses and will lead God's people into the land God had promised.

> *The Lord had said to Abram, "Go from your country, your people and your father's household to the land I will show you. I will make you into a great nation, and I will bless you; I will make your name great, and you will be a blessing. I will bless those who bless you, and whoever curses you I will curse; and all peoples on earth will be blessed through you."*
>
> —Gen. 12:1–3

Then God reiterates the promise about land (Gen. 15:7, 17:8 and many other places).

Do you remember the major themes? Land, seed, and blessing.

The book of Joshua is about God's people conquering the people who inhabit the Promised Land so they can take possession of it just like God had promised. That is where we see the story of Rahab the harlot in Jericho.

Jericho is the first city the Israelites conquer. The spies go in, and Rahab hides them and asks them to remember her. The only people spared in Jericho are Rahab and her family. We will come back to her in a bit.

The book of Joshua is the conquest of the Promised Land through battles where God's people conquer the pagans who live in the land God has promised His people.

After Joshua dies, there is no one to take over for him. Thus we enter the period of judges.

Some scholars have said that the book of Joshua is about the conquest of Canaan, and the book of Judges is about the Canaanization of the Israelites. Canaanization is a made-up word that shows how God's people start to act more like pagans than people who are following God's Law and worshiping him.

> *The book of Joshua is about the conquest of Canaan, but the book of Judges is about the Canaanization of the Israelites.*

The book of Judges immediately begins with God's people starting to go downhill, and it just gets worse. In fact, some of the most appalling stories in the Bible are found in the book of Judges. As you read this book, it goes from bad to worse.

There is a consistent cycle that happens over and over. It is called the Cycle of Judges and goes like this:

- God's people fall into idolatry and sin.

- They are conquered or suffer greatly through bondage or slavery.

- Sometime later they repent and ask God to redeem them.

- God raises up a judge and restores the nation.

- Very quickly they fall right back into sin and idolatry.

And again, it goes from bad to worse. The book ends with these terrible words: "In those days Israel had no king; everyone did as they saw fit" (Judges 21:25).

Some translations say they did what was right in their own eyes. And it led to deep, deep darkness. It led them away from the promises of God that Moses and Joshua had led them in.

That begs the question: What is God going to do? He has made all kinds of promises. He has promised that if God's people follow Him, blessing will follow. If they don't, they will be cursed. There is supposed to be a descendant who conquers the enemy. What is God going to do? We enter the period of the kings.

Kings

In 1 Samuel and 2 Samuel, we transition from judges to kings. Samuel is the last judge (1 Sam. 7:6, 15–17). He was also a prophet of God (Acts 3:24). He is the leader of God's people who go to him and demand a king (1 Sam. 8:20). God tells Samuel to give them what they want, even though it will end badly. The first king of Israel is a man named Saul.

During Saul's reign, Samuel actually anoints David as the next king. It is fascinating because we all know that God is ushering in David who will be the greatest king Israel ever has.

If we were to pause and go back to the small book of Ruth between the books of Judges and 1 Samuel, we see something incredible. In the timeline of the world, the events of the book of Ruth happen during the time of judges and before the reign of Saul.

The book of Ruth tells about a Moabite woman who marries into a Jewish family. Her husband dies, but she continues to serve her mother-in-law. In the course of time, a Jewish man named Boaz marries her, and they have a family. Here's how the book of Ruth ends.

This, then, is the family line of Perez: Perez was the father of Hezron, Hezron the father of Ram, Ram the father of Amminadab, Amminadab the father of Nahshon, Nahshon the father of Salmon, Salmon the father of Boaz, Boaz the father of Obed, Obed the father of Jesse, and Jesse the father of David.

—Ruth 4:18–22

Do you remember the father of Perez? It was Judah. Here is another fun fact. Do you know the name of Boaz's mother (Matt. 1:5)? It was Rahab from the story of the fall of Jericho in Joshua 2 and 6. In the chapter on Genesis, We saw that God's promise to have a descendant who conquers Satan goes from Abraham to Isaac to Jacob to Judah to Perez to Boaz and on down to David. Even though the world was crazy, and the period of judges was dark, God was still at work in the background bringing all His promises to fulfillment.

Let's go back to the kings in 1 and 2 Samuel. We are approximately 600 years removed from Abraham, and God is at work. God is faithful, even when His people are not. Now we come to David.

David is the one who bravely fought Goliath. The whole Israelite army is scared on the mountainside, but David trusts in God. With one stone and one toss of his sling, Goliath falls.

This is the David who the people sang songs about—about slaying his ten thousands. He is the writer of many of the psalms. He is not perfect by any means, but the Bible says he is a man after God's own heart (1 Sam. 13:14).

It is this David who will reign supreme and firmly establish the kingdom of Israel. They will follow God, and He will bless them like crazy. God will promise that David will always have a descendant on the throne.

> *Even though the world has been crazy, and the period of judges was dark, God was still at work in the background bringing all His promises to fulfillment.*

The Lord declares to you that the Lord himself will establish a house for you: When your days are over and you rest with your ancestors, I will raise up your offspring to succeed you, your own flesh and blood, and I will establish his kingdom. He is the one who will build a house for my Name, and I will establish the throne of his kingdom forever. I will be his father, and he will be my son. When he does wrong, I will punish him with a rod wielded by men, with floggings inflicted by human hands. But my love will never be taken away from him, as I took it away from Saul, whom I removed from before you. Your house and your kingdom will endure forever before me; your throne will be established forever.

—2 Sam. 7:11–16

And one day, God's fullest promises will somehow come through the line of David. But how? Watch how the story continues.

Solomon, Rehoboam, Split Kingdom

After David, his son Solomon takes over. Solomon is the wisest king who ever lived. He wrote much of the Proverbs, the Song of Songs, and Ecclesiastes. He followed in David's footsteps until the end of his life when he got a little crazy, but he enjoyed the overwhelming prosperity of God. He built the permanent Temple in Jerusalem, so God no longer dwelled in a portable tent, the Tabernacle. He did incredible things, and the kingdom flourished like never before.

When Solomon dies, his son Rehoboam takes over (1

Kings 12 and 2 Chron. 10). The people come to Rehoboam and ask him to lighten the load that Solomon put on them. Rehoboam asks for three days to seek wisdom.

In those three days he talks to the elders, the ones who helped guide Solomon. They encourage him to lighten the load and serve the people well. Rehoboam then turns and talks to his buddies. They instruct him to be harsh and impose even heavier loads upon the people.

When the people come back in three days for an answer, Rehoboam answers them harshly. This is a very significant moment in understanding the Old Testament. This is the moment when Israel becomes a divided kingdom. Ten of the 12 tribes go with a man named Jeroboam. This is the northern kingdom, or Israel. The tribe of Judah and Benjamin are left with Rehoboam as their king (1 Kings 12:20). This is the southern kingdom, or Judah.

There are now two kingdoms—Israel and Judah. They will each have their own kings. The kings of Judah are descendants of David. Israel's kings are not.

Without fail, the kings of Israel all do evil in God's sight. That means they follow the gods of the pagan nations instead of following the one true God. Those gods were the Baals and the Ashtoreths and Chemosh and many other so-called gods listed throughout the Old Testament.

This is the context and setting for the lives of some of our most famous prophets such as Elijah and Elisha. Israel's worship of pagans is the setting for one of my favorite stories—Elijah and the 450 prophets of Baal (1 Kings 18). God's people are speaking against the pagan Israelite rulers because those kings are not following God.

All the kings of Israel did evil, but the kings of Judah were different. Some of the kings of Judah did what was evil in God's sight, and some did what was right.

One reason 2 Kings and 2 Chronicles are hard to read is because they are telling the story of two different kingdoms and all their kings at the exact same time chronologically. Some of those kings from each nation overlap each other, which can get confusing.

Israel's Exile

Remember what God promised in Deuteronomy 28 if His people rebel? He promised that He would allow other nations to conquer them and scatter them. That is what is about to happen in the story of the world.

The Assyrians come first. They invade Israel and conquer it in 722 BC. They deport many Israelites and take them into exile. Second Kings 17 explains the Assyrian exile and all of Israel's wickedness. God allows the Assyrians to conquer God's people because He is fulfilling His own words from Deuteronomy 28.

Side note: the nation of Assyria are pagans. The book of Jonah details how God calls Jonah to go and preach to Ninevah, which is the capital of Assyria. It also helps us understand why Jonah ran. He did not want to go and preach to these pagan people. Jonah gets a bad rap for hating the Ninevites, but we would too. God decides to teach us so much through Jonah.

He shows us that He loves people, even pagan people. We see God calming the storm after Jonah is cast into the sea and the sailors are saved. We see God sending the fish to swallow Jonah, who then repents and goes to preach in Nineveh. We see God's grace that is so patient with Jonah even after Jonah throws a fit that God doesn't overthrow Nineveh. That gives a fuller context to Jonah because the people he is preaching to are the same people who have done so much harm to his own people. I love teaching the story of Jonah, but we have to keep moving.

Judah's Exile

Remember, the nation is divided. The northern kingdom, Israel, is conquered by the Assyrians in 722 BC. The southern kingdom, Judah, will be conquered by the Babylonians, but it will be a bit later. The Babylonians conquer the Assyrians and then continue to expand, setting their eyes on Judah.

It may seem harsh to think that God is allowing His people to be conquered. Not only did God predict this in Deuteronomy 28, but before, during, and after the pagans are invading God's territory, God is constantly sending His prophets to warn everyone.

He sends His prophets to compel people to change, repent, and follow God. They are Isaiah, Jeremiah, Ezekiel, Daniel, and more. God's people just don't seem to listen to God's prophets.

As the story goes, the last king of Judah who did right in the eyes of God is at the same time Israel gets deported (722 BC). Then, for a little over 100 years, there is a series of kings of Judah who do not do what is right in the eyes of God.

God's people in Judah will be conquered and deported at least two times. The first one is when the Babylonians take all the best and brightest people back to Babylon to try to brainwash them and assimilate them into the Babylonian culture. This is the fuller context of the book of Daniel.

Here's another little fun bit of info. If you read the last half of Daniel, you'll see that Daniel predicts everything I am about to tell you. He describes events that had already happened—the Assyrians conquering the Israelites, the Babylonians conquering the Assyrians, the Persians conquering the Babylonians. Daniel also prophesies that in the future, the Greeks, with Alexander the Great, are going to conquer the Persians. Then the Romans are going to overthrow the Greeks. By the time of Jesus, it is the Romans who control this territory. But I am getting ahead of myself.

So there are several exiles of the people of Judah. After the first exile, they left a king in charge, but basically, he was a puppet. He was ruling, but the Babylonians were really in charge. Judah is not thriving and barely hanging on. They are paying tributes and barely surviving.

The last king of Judah, King Zedekiah, tries to rebel against the Babylonians. That is when the Babylonians come in and

clean house (see how 2 Chronicles and 2 Kings end). It is actually
quite terrible.

> *In 586 BC, the
> Babylonians tear
> down the walls of
> Jerusalem.*

King Zedekiah rebels, and
then the Babylonians invade and
sack Jerusalem. They murder all of
Zedekiah's kids right in front of him. Then they pluck out his
eyes so the last thing he sees is the death of his children. Awful!
What also makes this so devastating is that in 586 BC, the
Babylonians tear down the walls of Jerusalem. They literally
tear down the Temple. They devastate and plunder and leave
Jerusalem in utter ruin.

It is a big deal to us, but it was even a bigger deal for the
Jewish people. Jerusalem was the center of their worship. It was
where God's presence had once dwelt. It had hundreds of years
of meaning. Not only that, but God had promised them this
land. How could they be conquered?

Let's finish the story of the Old Testament.

The Rest of the Old Testament

In the course of time—in 539 BC—Persia will conquer the
Babylonians. This is important because it is the Persian kings
who allow some of God's people to return to Jerusalem.

A group of minor prophets, including Haggai and Zepha-
niah, are writing in this time. More famously, we have stories
from Ezra, Nehemiah, and Esther.

Ezra tells the story of how God's people got permission to

return to Judah from their Babylonian exile and rebuild of the Temple in Jerusalem.

Nehemiah tells how God's people got permission and completed the rebuilding of the walls around Jerusalem. Nehemiah tells the story of the Old Testament (see Nehemiah 9).

Esther is the story of how a Jewish woman becomes queen of Persia and saves the Jewish people from annihilation. It is also the story that gives the Jewish people the festival of Purim, which kind of looks like America's Halloween.

> *Nehemiah tells the story of the Old Testament (see Nehemiah 9).*

The Old Testament ends with the book of Malachi.

One of the themes that runs throughout the prophets is that one day God will restore what was broken and torn down. There are themes of a suffering servant. There are themes of an anointed one coming to rescue, redeem, and restore. God will somehow save a remnant, and they will be His people, and He will be their God.

After Malachi, there are 400 years of silence when God almost seems gone.

There is no more writing of the Bible or gaining revelation from God.

That's true until the moment the angel comes to John the Baptist's dad. Then the angel comes to Mary. Then on that one night that Jesus is born, the creation and the heavens explode in praise because God is still at work fulfilling everything He has ever promised.

SMALL GROUP QUESTIONS

1. What was the significance of the first Passover? What happened, and what recurring theme do you see?

2. The chapter stated, "If God is just, He must deal with our sin." What are the implications if God does not deal with sin? How do you think God is going to deal with sin in the future (foreshadowing)?

3. How would you summarize the Old Testament in one sentence? Do you know of specific examples that show this?

4. What is revealed at the end of the book of Ruth? How does this tie together Genesis to 1 Samuel?

5. What year was Israel conquered and by whom? What year was Judah conquered and by whom? Knowing these details is important to understand much of the Old Testament.

Chapter 6

WHAT IS THE BIBLE ABOUT?

Metanarrative Part 4:
The Good News

If we had to summarize the Old Testament, we would say that there is repeated evidence of the sinfulness of humanity. Even though God's people were rebellious and sinful, God is repeatedly faithful. He gives them chance after chance for hundreds of years. He makes a way for them to come into His presence. His heart is that He wants His people to know Him. Even so, the Old Testament does not end with God's people flourishing.

If we were to honestly assess our lives, we would come to the conclusion that we are much more like the Israelites than we may want to admit. We complain, grumble, doubt God, fail to honor God, turn our backs on God, and more. We do the exact same things as the people in the Old Testament.

If we were really honest, we know that we deserve the same slavery, bondage, wrath of God, and punishment that they received.

As we have seen all throughout this metanarrative, the heart of God is not to leave us in our sin, slavery, and bondage. God has always had a plan, and the hero is about to be born. His name is Jesus. This is the gospel.

It is the best news in the world.

> *God has always had a plan, and the hero is about to be born. His name is Jesus.*

New Testament

When you get to the New Testament, the first four books are called the Gospels. They give an account of the life, death, burial, and resurrection of Jesus. The rest of the New Testament deals with the church that Jesus institutes. It is all so interesting and of utmost importance to us.

Let's start with Jesus. If you have an understanding of what I have written in the last few chapters, then it changes the way you read Matthew 1. Normally, we skip genealogies. When you understand the promises of God in Genesis 3 and 12 and see how God's promise has been passing from generation to generation throughout the Old Testament, then Jesus's

> *Read Matthew 1. How many of the names do you recognize from earlier in the story?*

genealogy becomes awesome. Read Matthew 1. How many of the names do you recognize from earlier in the story?

With that in mind, let's think about Jesus's birth, life, death, and resurrection.

Birth

When you hear the Christmas story, it is rarely with the excitement it deserves. We have heard the story and read the Scriptures so many times that we can easily fail to wonder at its glory.

For over a thousand years, God's people had been waiting for this person, this anointed one, this Messiah to enter the world. In Genesis 3, we learned that this person will crush Satan. Throughout the Old Testament, there are hints and prophecies predicting this person.

The angel comes to Mary and tells her she is going to be pregnant. But how? She cannot possibly be pregnant. She is a virgin (Isa. 7:14). This is no ordinary pregnancy. It is a supernatural conception (Matt. 1:18–19). This is not just any baby. He will be the Savior of the world.

On the night of Jesus's birth (Luke 2:1–21), there are no rooms available at the inn. Mary and Joseph are literally teenagers in a barn with animals and no doctor. It is gross and dirty. It is no place for a woman to give birth, much less a place for the Son of God to enter the world.

There are shepherds out in a field. It is dark. There are no streetlights or other lights. It is pitch black. Then all of a sudden, brightness and angels appear, declaring the birth of Jesus. Have you ever been startled? I can't imagine how high the shepherds jumped when not only someone appears out of nowhere, but it is a heavenly being.

And what happens? They are glorifying and celebrating. The long-anticipated Messiah is born! If this were a movie, the music would be swelling. We have been leading up to this moment for so long, and Jesus is here! He is God who has put on flesh. He is the Savior of the world. He is our hope!

The theological word for this is *incarnation*. Jesus was not created by Mary. No, Jesus has always been. In Genesis 1, Jesus is already there. He has no beginning or end. This Jesus who is part of the Godhead chooses to step out of heaven and put on human flesh to dwell

> **Incarnation** *is the theological word to help us understand how God (Jesus) put on flesh and dwelled among us.*

among us. There is mystery here. God is 100 percent God and 100 percent human at the same time. Fascinating. This is the incarnation (Phil. 2:5–11).

Life

Jesus really lived. He was hungry and thirsty (Mark 11:12, John 4:7). He got tired (Matt. 8:23–27). He had friends and enemies. He had happy and sad moments. He was like us.

He also had brothers and sisters (Matt. 13:55–56). After Jesus was born, Mary and Joseph had other children. It seems that somewhere along the way, Joseph dies. After Jesus's 12th birthday (Luke 2:41–52), there is no more mention of Joseph. Jesus experienced the ups and downs of life.

Even though Jesus was fully human, He lived a perfect, sinless life. He never sinned (1 Cor. 5:21). He was 100 percent God. Even though He was God in the flesh, He was tempted in every way that we are, yet He never failed (Heb. 4:15). Jesus was perfectly pure. In every situation and moment, Jesus lived according to how God had designed life to be lived.

Jesus healed the sick (Mark 1:32), calmed the storm (Mark 4:35–41), and raised dead people to life (John 11:38–44). He opened deaf ears (Mark 7:31–37) and made the blind to see (Mark 8:22–25). No demon could withstand him (Mark 5:1–20). Jesus walked in the authority of the Creator God.

I have heard it said that it is incredible to see Jesus who perfectly represented God on earth. Thinking of this in another way, it is also incredible to think that God is like Jesus. Jesus lived the life that we were intended to live in Genesis 1–2. He shows us God's heart, intentions, and hopes. He shows us what true life is. He is pure, perfect, and whole.

Death and Burial

Jesus's perfection is one of many reasons that His death is so fascinating. He does not deserve to die, but He does. His death is deeply beautiful.

Think about it. The Sunday before Jesus's death, He entered Jerusalem on a donkey (John 12:12–16). This is called Palm Sunday. The crowds were laying down palm branches as

He entered and saying "Hosanna," which basically means "God save us."

Jesus spends the week going in and out of the Temple, teaching and being present. On Thursday, Jesus has the Last Supper with His disciples to celebrate Passover (John 13–17 gives much detail

The Lord's Supper, or communion, includes bread that represents Jesus's broken body and juice that represents His shed blood for us.

about Jesus's last night before His death). This is the meal that Jewish people had been celebrating for a thousand years where they killed and ate a Passover lamb to commemorate the Exodus from Egypt.

At this meal on Thursday night, Jesus institutes the Lord's Supper (Mark 14:22–26). This is the ordinance the church observes by breaking the bread and taking juice to remember the broken body and shed blood of Jesus. On this night, Jesus is teaching His disciples that ultimately, the Passover is about Him. He is the Passover lamb that takes away the sins of the world. This meal will now be taken to a whole new level because it will be a celebration to remember Jesus and all He did.

From this room where this meal was shared, Jesus leads His disciples, minus Judas, to the Garden of Gethsemane. Judas leaves mid-supper and is planning to betray Jesus.

In the Garden of Gethsemane, Jesus prays to His Father three times. The Bible says it is such intense prayer that Jesus sweats drops of blood (Luke 2:44). Jesus had predicted at least three times leading up to this moment that He would be going to the cross (Matt. 16:21–23, 17:22–23, 20:17–19). Hours before it happens, He is asking God the Father to allow it to pass. I believe Jesus prays this because He understands the eternal weight of what

> *If God is going to rescue and redeem sinners once and for all, then the sinless Lamb of God must be slain.*

He is walking into. But it is God's will. There is no other way. If God is going to rescue and redeem sinners once and for all, then the sinless Lamb of God must be slain.

It is in this Garden as Jesus is praying that Judas comes with the band of soldiers to betray Jesus and hand him over to the Roman guards (Luke 22:47–53). Jesus is taken and falsely accused. There is injustice everywhere. His arrest is illegal. He hasn't done anything wrong. The trials are illegal. They purposefully get people to testify lies about Jesus. It is insane (Matt. 26:57–60).

Jesus stands before Caiaphus, the high priest, and the religious leaders. Caiaphus asks Jesus if He is the Messiah, and Jesus tells him He is. Caiaphus says this is blasphemy, rips his own clothes, and condemns Jesus to death (Matt. 26:61–68).

During these false trials, Peter, who had told Jesus he would die for Him, denies Him three times (Matt. 26:69–75). Jesus is then sent to Pilate, the Roman governor, to be put to death.

Pilate, in talking to Jesus, finds no fault in Him. The same crowd who shouted "Hosanna" last Sunday is shouting "Crucify Him" on Friday morning. Pilate tries to get out of it, but the crowd presses on. Pilate gives in and hands Jesus over to the guards (Matt. 27:11–26).

Jesus has been up all night. He has been falsely accused, hit, and spit on. The Roman soldiers slam a crown of thorns into Jesus's skull. They put a purple robe on Him and mockingly bow before Him. They lead Jesus to be flogged. His hands are tied up, exposing His bare back, and the Roman guards lash Him with whips that have thorns, bones, and glass tied to the ends. They were used for the sole purpose of inflicting the most extreme pain (John 19:1–3).

After the flogging, Jesus is forced to carry His own cross to His death, but Jesus isn't strong enough and has to have help (Matt. 27:32).

When Jesus finally gets to Golgotha, the guards stretch Him across two wooden beams. They drive a large nail through each of His hands to fasten Him to the wood. Then they cross His feet and put another nail through them (John 19:16–18).

As they raise the wooden cross, it thuds into the premade hole. The Savior of the world hangs suspended in the air. His back is raw from wounds. His face is bloody from punches and thorns. He is almost naked in the cool of the morning. It is 9:00 on the morning we call Good Friday (Mark 15:25).

From noon until 3:00 p.m., darkness falls over the whole land (Mark 15:33). It isn't cloudy; it is a supernatural darkness. There is something supernatural happening on the cross. Jesus isn't just dying. He is bearing the wrath of God for our sins. A cosmic, eternal battle is happening.

When Jesus says, "My God, my God, why have you forsaken me?" (Mark 15:34), I believe He is articulating that for the first and only time in the history of the world, God the Father and the Son, who live in perfect harmony, are being separated as Jesus becomes sin for

> *Jesus isn't just dying. He is bearing the wrath of God for our sins. A cosmic, eternal battle is happening.*

us (2 Cor. 5:21). I think this was worse than all the physical pain. Our sin, for a moment, tore the Son from the Father.

At 3:00 p.m. (Mark 15:33), Jesus says, "It is finished" and gives up His spirit. Why? Because the mission was accomplished. The payment for our sin was complete. Jesus did all He had set out to do. When it was finished, He gave up His spirit.

A man named Joseph of Arimethea hears that Jesus is dead. He goes to Pilate and asks for Jesus's body, and Pilate grants his request (Mark 15:42–47). Joseph gets Jesus's body and takes it to his own tomb, a tiny cave carved into the side of a mountain, just big enough for a person to be buried there.

He puts Jesus in the tomb and rolls the stone over the entrance. That is how Friday ends. The Lamb of God has been slaughtered.

Resurrection

The Jewish Sabbath begins at sundown on Friday and goes to sundown on Saturday. Can you imagine how that Saturday must have felt?

Peter has denied Christ. I am sure he is filled with more shame and regret than I can imagine.

All the disciples, save John (John 19:26–27), scattered when Jesus was taken. What are they thinking on Saturday?

All of Jesus's followers assumed that the Messiah was going to restore the nation of Israel to its rightful place as a nation of dominance. There were so many prophecies that seemed to hint that the Messiah was going to restore the nation of Israel to prominence like in the days of David and Solomon (Isa. 11:11–12, Jer. 23:5–8, Hosea 3:4–5). Jesus is dead. The movement must be over. But how? It was filled with the miraculous, things that only God can do. It seemed like Jesus truly was the Messiah. How could He be dead?

It had to be the longest Saturday in the history of the world.

That Sunday morning, the women are headed to the tomb. They are bringing spices (Luke 24:1). Why? Because Jesus's body was not properly anointed before He was put in the tomb, and they are planning to do the ceremonial anointing of His body.

> *It had to be the longest Saturday in the history of the world.*

When they arrive, they realize the stone is rolled away. The angel declares, "He is not here; he has risen!" (Luke 24:6). This is the first Easter Sunday (Luke 24:1–8).

The fact that Jesus did not stay dead is the most important detail in all of Christianity. It is the main thing that separates Jesus from anyone who has ever had any kind of religious following or teaching. Every major prophet or cult leader has died and stayed dead. Jesus died as a sacrifice, but the grave could not hold Him. Praise be to God!

Application

This is the gospel in story form. I want to explain doctrinally why it is the best news in the entire world.

Remember, God created us to know Him closely. However, we are all sinners, which separates us from God. This is the biggest issue every person who has ever lived faces.

Because of Jesus, we can turn from our sin and put our faith and trust in God. We believe Jesus and receive His sacrifice for the forgiveness of our sins. We have undersold this idea too often. We are not simply repeating a prayer. This idea of turning from our sin to trust and follow Jesus has cosmic ramifications.

Romans 10:9–10 says, "If you declare with your mouth, 'Jesus is Lord,' and believe in your heart that God raised him from the dead, you will be saved. For it is with your heart that you believe and are justified, and it is with your mouth that you profess your faith and are saved." When you do what these verses say, you are literally laying your life down. This is not repeating some words and nothing changing in your life.

> *Christianity is a surrendering of yourself. We are laying our lives at Jesus's feet, trusting in His sacrifice on our behalf.*

Christianity is a surrendering of yourself. We are laying our lives at Jesus's feet, trusting in His sacrifice on our behalf, and asking God to use our lives as He sees fit.

When someone puts their faith in Jesus, all kinds of things happen. It is truly miraculous.

What are some results?

Our sin is atoned for.

When Jesus died for us on the cross, He made atonement, or payment, for our sin (1 John 2:1–2). And He paid our bill in full. Jesus is the ultimate innocent dying for the guilty! Innocent blood covers a guilty soul. Innocent lambs die for the transgressions of God's people.

> *Jesus is the ultimate innocent dying for the guilty!*

When Jesus died, it was not because He was guilty of sin (2 Cor. 5:21). He was innocent. He was not just innocent; He was sinless and perfectly pure. He was spotless and without blemish like the animals were supposed to be when they were sacrificed in the Tabernacle (Exod. 12:5).

The payment for our sin was death (Rom. 6:23). Because of our sin, we deserve to die, but Jesus is our innocent substitute. He is spotless and an acceptable sacrifice.

> *Jesus is the only innocent person who has ever lived, and He willingly laid down His life so we might live.*

Jesus is the only innocent person who has ever lived, and He willingly laid down His life so we might live (John 10:17–18).

I often ask my students if they could die for their own sins and make the necessary payment. Answers vary, but the biblical answer is no. We cannot fully pay for our own sins because we are not an acceptable sacrifice.

This is also why it seems that hell is an eternal payment for our sins. Either Jesus can pay for our sins as our substitute on the cross or we can pay for them in eternity separated from God (the definition of hell). If an eternity separated from God seems like a steep payment for sin, that goes to show that sin is way worse than we tend to think.

> *When we put our faith in Christ, we are adopted into God's family. This is an act where God makes us members of His family—His sons and daughters now and forever.*

The following terms help us more fully understand how our sin is dealt with and what our new relationship with Jesus is like. Justification means we are instantly and legally (1) forgiven of our sins, past, present, and future, and have taken on Christ's righteousness; and (2) declared to be right by the blood of Jesus in God's eyes (Rom. 3:21–26, Col. 1:21–22, 2 Cor. 5:21).

We also receive expiation. That means we are cleansed from sin, both the sins we have committed and the sins that have been committed against us through Christ's work on the cross (1 John 1:7).

Jesus's sacrifice is also a propitiation for our sin. That is a sacrifice that bears God's wrath to the end and in so doing changes God's wrath toward us to His favor (1 John 4:10).

We also receive imputation. We are credited with Christ's

righteousness. Jesus took God's wrath for me and in turn gave me His righteousness (2 Cor. 5:21).

When we put our faith in Christ, we are adopted into God's family. This is an act where God makes us members of His family—His sons and daughters now and forever (Gal. 4:4–7).

All the previous doctrinal items happen instantly when we become believers.

Sanctification is a progressive work that makes us more and more free from sin and more like Christ in our actual lives (1 Thess. 5:23).

Through Jesus, we now have access to God. Remember the Tabernacle and the Temple? There was an outer court, inner court,

How do we come back into the presence of a holy and just God? By being covered by the blood of Jesus!

and Holy of Holies. Only the High Priest could go behind the veil into the Holy of Holies once per year on the Day of Atonement. When Jesus gave up His spirit, the veil blocking the Holy of Holies was supernaturally ripped in half (Matt. 27:51). Because of this, the writer of Hebrews encourages us to come boldly to the throne of grace so we might receive help in time of need (Heb. 4:16). God *wants* us to be in His presence.

Our access to God is through Jesus, our mediator (1 Tim. 2:5). We have a new way to relate to God. Jesus is our Great High Priest (Heb. 4:14–16).

Our access to God is through Jesus by the power of the Holy Spirit. When we truly put our faith in Jesus, God gives us the Holy Spirit. In the Old Testament, God's presence rested in the Tabernacle and later in the Temple. Now our bodies are the new Temple of God where God's holy presence dwells (1 Cor. 6:19).

What a mighty God we serve! What incredible benefits God bestows on us by grace!

I feel urged to apologize for the brevity of this last section. It truly deserves much more explanation and illustration. Entire books are written about what I wrote in brief about the application of the gospel. I barely scratched the surface. Truly, during our lives and into eternity, we will be marveling at the wondrous work of God in and through Jesus Christ. Praise be to God!

The Rest of the New Testament

God is the main character of the Bible, and Jesus is the hero. Jesus's resurrection is not the end of the story. Jesus institutes the church. When He leaves, He gives a charge to His disciples in Matthew 28. This is called the Great Commission.

> *Then Jesus came to them and said, "All authority in heaven and on earth has been given to me. Therefore go and make disciples of all nations, baptizing them in the name of the Father and of the Son and of the Holy Spirit, and teaching them to obey everything I have commanded you. And surely I am with you always, to the very end of the age."*
>
> —Matt. 28:18–20

The disciples, who were so idiotic during Jesus's life and so cowardly during Jesus's death, are now very different. Almost every disciple of Jesus (there are 11 at this point in the story because Judas Iscariot hung himself after he betrayed Jesus) will die because they will refuse to recant their faith in Jesus.

> *What would have to happen to make guys who were so cowardly be willing to give up their lives? They saw the risen Lord.*

What would have to happen to make 11 guys who were so cowardly be willing to give up their lives? They saw the risen Lord. Jesus's resurrection changes everything.

Look at the last moments of Jesus's earthly life.

> *Then they gathered around him and asked him, "Lord, are you at this time going to restore the kingdom to Israel?" He said to them: "It is not for you to know the times or dates the Father has set by his own authority. But you will receive power when the Holy Spirit comes on you; and you will be my witnesses in Jerusalem, and in all Judea and Samaria, and to the ends of the earth."*
>
> —Acts 1:6–8

See? They really thought the Messiah was going to restore the nation of Israel. He had much bigger, more eternal plans.

The church of Jesus is the people who have put their faith in Jesus. Church is not a building. It has always been a people. On Sundays, the church gathers for worship (we do not go to church; we are the church).

In this passage, Jesus says His people are going to receive the Spirit and then be His witnesses. And as His witnesses, they will spread His message to the ends of the earth.

In the next verse, Jesus ascends into heaven as His followers watch. The rest of the book of Acts is the story of how the message of Jesus spreads to Jerusalem, Judea, Samaria, and the ends of the earth.

In Acts, we will see Peter become a pillar of the church in Jerusalem. His main mission is to preach the good news to the Jewish people.

We will also be introduced to a guy named Paul who will be a missionary to the Gentiles.

Much of the New Testament (Romans to Jude) are letters written to various churches or Christians throughout the known world during the first century. They contain teachings about Jesus and the church. They give encouragement, correction, and guidance to Christians who are following Jesus. They give warnings and predictions and so much more.

The last book of the Bible—Revelation—tells of the end times and the reality that Jesus will not only return but His people will be with Him for all eternity.

Conclusion

I hope and pray that you can see how so much of Jesus's life is informed by an understanding of the Old Testament. The more you understand the Old Testament, the more you understand the New Testament. But I want to show you one more thing.

Do you remember how we started? In Chapter 1, we said the Bible is not about you but is absolutely for you. Do you remember that? Then I told you the 30,000-foot version of the story in Chapters 3 through 6. We spent a lot of time poring over many of the details in the Old and New Testaments.

But there is something I didn't tell you specifically. Every time you read a story in the Old Testament, you are reading more than one story, but it is the same story.

Think about it. The overarching story of the Bible is this story of God. But in the details of that story of God, you have all these other characters, stories, and happenings. So when you read a story in the Old Testament, you are reading more than one story at a time.

So yes, we can read just about Joseph and what he experienced. There are many lessons to learn from Joseph's life, but there is a deeper story than just some lessons about how to deal with hardship. The story of Joseph shows us how God is carrying out His promises through Israel's fourthborn son, Judah. Brilliant!

> *When you read a story in the Old Testament, you are reading more than one story at a time.*

But there is more, so much more.

Layer one is the immediate story you read. Layer two is how that story fits into God's big story. Layer three is how it is all about Jesus. This third layer changes everything.

After Jesus resurrects, there is a story in Luke 24 where He is on the road to Emmaus. He meets two guys, and they

begin having a conversation about the Christ who was crucified. They have no idea they are talking to Jesus.

But notice how Jesus responds. "And beginning with
Moses and all the Prophets, he explained to them what was
said in all the Scriptures concerning himself" (Luke 24:27).

The Bible is about God's grand
story of redemption through Jesus.
The Bible is about all these Bible
characters and how they play a part
in that redemption. But even more
so, the Bible is about Jesus.

> *Every story in the
> Old Testament is a
> story within a story.
> Every story fits into
> God's grand story of
> redemption.*

The third layer you are constantly reading about is the fore-
shadowing of who the One predicted in Genesis 3 will be—the
One who will crush Satan. It is Jesus. And all along the way,
you have hints and foreshadowings of the coming Messiah.

Think about the story of David and Goliath. When you
read that story, you can apply it to giants in your life, but
there's a deeper story than that. This story sits in a specific context with the nation of Israel in the midst of God's grand story.
Not only that, but it is also a foreshadowing. One day there
will be One who comes and conquers the greatest giant the
world has ever seen—sin, death, and hell.

Every story in the Old Testament is a story within a story.
Every story fits into God's grand story of redemption. I would
give almost anything to have been there that day on the road
to Emmaus listening to Jesus preach about Jesus from the Old
Testament. Can you imagine?

The story isn't just about redemption; it is about Jesus. And in every way, the Old Testament is pointing to and foreshadowing Jesus. The more you study, the more you will see Jesus. The more you see Jesus, the more you will worship.

The Bible is not about you, but it is absolutely for you. Because the Bible is about Jesus, we benefit for eternity.

With all this in mind, read these verses, knowing the big story makes these verses even more meaningful.

He redeemed us in order that the blessing given to Abraham might come to the Gentiles through Christ Jesus, so that by faith we might receive the promise of the Spirit.

—Gal. 3:14

This mystery is that through the gospel the Gentiles are heirs together with Israel, members together of one body, and sharers together in the promise in Christ Jesus.

—Eph. 3:6

This is how God relates to us. This is how a sinful people can be in the presence of a holy, sinless God. This is how we are forgiven and restored. This is how the curse is reversed. This is our hope—Jesus.

Restoration: Revelation 19-22

Previously, I said we could summarize the story of the Bible in four overarching ideas: Creation, Fall, Redemption, and Restoration.

One day God is going to finish what He began. He is going to restore the world to the way it was in the Garden of Eden. He will reign supreme. He will be glorified. We will spend forever with Him.

We can argue over the details, but the point is that Christ will return. Those He has redeemed will spend an eternity with Him. And it will be better than we can ever imagine.

Now that you have a basic understanding of the overarching story of the Bible, let's turn to learning how to read it in a way that is helpful. This is where the Bible will come to life, and I can't wait to show you.

──────────── **SMALL GROUP QUESTIONS** ────────────

1. What are the first four books of the New Testament, and what do they teach?

2. Did you read Matthew 1:1–17? How many names did you recognize on the list?

3. Define these words: incarnation, atonement, justification, expiation, propitiation, and imputation.

4. The chapter described what it means to become a Christian in the section called "Application." Is this how you understand what it means to be saved or become a Christian? If not, how would you explain how you become a Christian?

5. After reading this chapter, answer these questions we have been pondering.

   ☛ How is God going to fix the problem (the curse of sin)?

☞ How can sinful people come back into the presence of a
   holy, sinless God like He designed?

☞ If the world is broken, what hope do we have?

Chapter 7

HOW DO I READ THE BIBLE DEVOTIONALLY?

Do you get nervous, even just a little, when you meet someone new? I know it's not just me.

Next question. Do you ever get so focused on not messing up your name that you almost immediately forget the name of the person you just met? Isn't that the worst? It makes it so awkward later. Socially, there is a time period when it is appropriate to ask someone their name again. After a certain time, if you still don't know their name, you look really silly, and it can be super offensive.

So what do you do? You either fake it— "Heyyy, mannn"— or you go behind their back to someone who knows them and say, "Please, please remind me of their name, and don't tell them I asked."

I think this same idea can often happen in the church. You become a Christian or you start getting plugged in, and you are learning all kinds of new things. But sometimes, certain things don't stick properly. After a while, you feel really silly asking questions you feel you should know the answer to.

Sometimes churches just assume everyone knows what we mean when we say the things we say. When I talk about Jesus, I have to remind myself that everyone listening may not be

> *What if we didn't assume that everyone knows how to read the Bible devotionally?*

thinking the same things I am thinking, even though we are all thinking of the person of Jesus. When I say *saved* or *sin*, there may be different definitions of those terms out there.

Here is the assumption I want to focus on in this chapter, and it is a massive game-changer. What if we didn't assume that everyone knows how to read the Bible devotionally?

You know you should read the Bible. You may have heard many people talk about reading their Bible. Maybe you have been around long enough that you feel like you should already know how to do this, but for whatever reason, it is a struggle for you. This chapter will help.

When I was in high school, I began to try to take my faith seriously. I began hanging out with guys who were trying to live out their faith. We were still teenage boys, but it was leaps and bounds ahead of where I was before I hung out with them.

I remember reading through the book of Genesis for the first time. I grew up going to church every time the doors were open. I knew all the stories, but I had never read the whole book myself.

As I read it, I couldn't help but feel like the Sunday school teachers left out some really shady parts of Genesis. They filtered out some lying, cheating, and adultery.

What I really remember is that once I finished reading Genesis for the first time, I was super proud of myself. I told one of my older friends that I had finished reading all of Genesis. Kindly and with no sarcasm at all, he responded, "Awesome! What did you get out of it?" I didn't have an answer. My honest answer was that I finished it. I didn't know what I was doing or why.

That was my sophomore year of high school in 2001. Since that year, I have been trying to figure out how to read the Bible in such a way that I am growing in my relationship with the Lord. I don't want to read it just to read it, I want to read it and grow.

I started this book saying that the Bible is the primary way God has chosen to reveal Himself to mankind. I assume God could have chosen to reveal Himself however He wanted, but He chose His Word.

What we saw in creation and throughout the story is that God's heart is for us to know Him. This was His design with Adam and Eve. This was His plan through the Tabernacle and the Law. This is what Jesus made possible by paying for our sins and allowing us to be welcomed back into God's presence. God's heart is that He wants us to know Him. He has done everything necessary, including inspiring His Word and preserving it for us to this very day (see Chapter 2).

If this is true and we are serious about living the life God

has called us to live, we must learn
how to read His Word.

*God's heart is that
He wants us to
know Him.*

The problem is that we want it to be
easy and fast. We don't want a learning
curve. We don't want to wade through
the confusion. But almost anything we really want is gained slowly
and consistently over a long period of time. This is true of learning
how to read the Bible and our overall spiritual growth.

I am going to walk you through four overarching ideas or
principles that I believe will make your time in the Word more
beneficial.

Five Ideas or Principles

Commune Not Complete

This first idea is so important to remember. Spending specific
time reading your Bible is ultimately about communing with
the living God. We will get to reading plans in a minute, but
the temptation is to find a reading plan and complete it. Ultimately, you could complete a reading plan and not have your
heart transformed.

Our goal is not to complete a reading plan but to commune
with the living God. Remember, the overarching goal of our
existence and our very design from God is to know God and to
walk with Him all of our days. When it comes to reading the
Bible, we understand that this is one of the primary ways we
can know God and walk with Him all of our days. This is the
heart of this chapter.

However, this leads to many questions. Where do I start? What if I don't understand? Why can't I focus? Hopefully, this chapter will help with all these questions.

> *Our goal is not to complete a Bible reading plan but to commune with the living God.*

Choose a Translation

My prayer is that your heart's desire is to commune with the living God. The next thing you should check is your Bible translation. There are many Bible translations, and I am going to suggest a few.

The Old Testament was written in Hebrew, and the New Testament is in Greek and Aramaic. Scholars have translated these books into English, and there are three major ways they have done it.

Some translations are word for word. They take a Hebrew or Greek word and then find the best English word to convey the meaning of that word.

> *The Old Testament was written in Hebrew, and the New Testament is in Greek and Aramaic.*

Some translations are thought for thought. That usually helps it read easier. They have translated it in the hopes that we understand the overall message of the author's thoughts.

Some translations are paraphrased. These translations focus on getting the general idea across with clear language.

Word for word tends to be the most accurate but can be

difficult to read or understand in some places. Thought for thought tends to be more devotional and readable. Paraphrased versions are usually for newer believers or to gain a fresh perspective on a text.

Here are the most famous in each category:

- Word for Word – King James Version (KJV), English Standard Version (ESV), New American Standard Bible (NASB)

- Thought for Thought – New International Version (NIV), New Living Translation (NLT), Christian Standard Bible (CSB)

- Paraphrased – The Message (MSG)

If you don't know where to start, I suggest using your church's primary translation. If you don't have a church home, I suggest any of the thought for thought translations (NIV, NLT, CSB).

My personal favorite is the NIV, Journal the Word Bible. It is hard back with wide margins for taking notes. The paper is thicker than most Bibles. Check it out.

Create a Plan

Now you need to make a plan that works for you. You may ask what the best plan is. The best plan is whatever works for you. What works for you may not work for anyone else in the world, but if it works for you, that's a win. If you create a plan and it doesn't work, fix it.

For instance, if you commit to reading through the Bible in one year and you are suffocating and dread it every day, that plan isn't working. Find a plan that works for you and then make it better.

Here are some things to think through as you develop your plan.

Decide on a reading plan.

Decide what you are going to read in advance. There is a massive amount of content in the Bible but start somewhere.

Sometimes we finally sit down to read the Bible and feel lost. Where do I start? Some of us do the random flip. We just open the Bible and land on Song of Songs 4:5, "Your breasts are like two fawns, like twin fawns of a gazelle that browse among the lilies." What? How am I supposed to read that devotionally? The random flip can be awkward.

> *Find a plan that works for you and then make it better.*

I find it better to pick a reading plan in advance so when you spend time with God, you know exactly what you need to be reading.

Here are some suggestions for actual Bible reading plans:

- Read through a book of the Bible. Pick a book and read a chapter a day.

- Study a person in the Bible. Study the life of Moses, David, or the Apostles Paul or John.

- Study a specific topic such as fear, anxiety, or faith. Survey the Bible to see all it has to say about that topic.

- Use a daily devotional or the YouVersion Bible App. There are thousands of daily devotionals at your fingertips.

- Read through the whole Bible.

There are hundreds of plans to help you. Find a plan that works well for you today. Knowing in advance what you are going to read will help you maximize your time.

Find a time and place.

Are you a morning person or a night person? Do you have time during your lunch hour? What time of day can you consistently engage with God? Again, plan this in advance, and then protect your day around the time that works best for you.

I suggest that you have a specific place to study. What is the physical location where you can spend time in God's Word? Where can you do that?

Remove Distractions

Time and place are very important, but another thing to think about is how you cannot be distracted. What is the time of day and the place where you can be undistracted to read the Word of God?

You may need to wake up early or stay up past the kids' bedtime. It may mean putting your phone on airplane mode or leaving it in another room. It may mean shutting your office door.

For me, I have to start my day in the Word before my kids wake up, sitting in my recliner in the front living room with a cup of coffee in my hand. That is about the only time my house is quiet and calm. It works for me. Find what works for you.

I suggest picking a time and place in advance and trying it. If it works, great. If it doesn't work, try something else until you find what works for you.

Please note that different seasons of your life will dramatically change your time in the Word. If you have a newborn in the house, it would be unrealistic to expect an uninterrupted hour every day. Marriage, kids, sports seasons, jobs,

> *What is the time of day and the place where you can be undistracted to read the Word of God?*

moving, holidays, and more will cause your life to change. Figure out what works for you in the season you are in and then make it better. When life changes, roll with it and make new plans.

The hope is that you will prioritize time in the Word because you know that is how you connect to the living God. And we are created to know Him!

Read More Slowly Than You Think You Should

It can be hard to understand parts of the Bible. It is also difficult because the enemy hates it when we read the Word. He wants you to be distracted. He wants you to read just to check off your reading plan list and move on. The enemy does not want you to read slowly and prayerfully and commune with God. He is going to fight you. So read slowly so you can digest the text.

Read slowly, and read a passage more than once. If your reading plan is so extensive that you can't slow down and read and reread certain sections of a passage, you may have bitten off too much per day.

Read slowly and prayerfully. Then read it again. Allow the Word of God to soak into your heart and mind. That will lead to massive spiritual growth and learning to discern the voice of God (it would take another book to fully explain that, so just trust me).

I like to read with a pen in hand and a physical Bible (not a phone app or an iPad). I underline as I read. That helps me stay focused because I can read a whole

> *Read slowly and prayerfully. Then read it again.*

chapter sometimes with my mind in another universe. Anyone else? I want to read slowly and prayerfully and really ask God to speak.

One Question to Ask

In the next chapter, I will give you a host of questions to think through. Those questions are more along the lines of deeper study. For this chapter, I want it to be as simple as possible.

When I think about reading devotionally, I am not reading to prepare for a sermon or teach a class. I am not reading with any objective other than to commune with God. So I ask only one main question: What one thing stood out the most? Why?

Sometimes we struggle to read too much and can't focus or process it all.

Sometimes we read too fast and miss what God is trying to say. When we slow down and read prayerfully, asking God for one thing to stand out to us, it usually yields helpful fruit.

Asking God to show you one thing gives you something to look for as you read. It also helps you begin to learn the prompting of the Holy Spirit. As you read, certain

> *What one thing stood out the most? Why?*

words, phrases, or ideas will stand out to you. They will stand out to you for a reason. Take note of that. This is usually God helping to grow, change, or encourage you.

When something stands out, write it down. I use the Evernote software to track my reading and the verse(s) or ideas that stood out to me. I have also used it to journal my thoughts and ideas. I keep my prayer list above my reading plan, so I see it every day. That works for me. You may want a real journal so you can write by hand. My handwriting is too terrible. Maybe you don't want to journal at all. Do what is best for you.

Full disclosure: Some mornings it feels like God is sitting next to me. It is incredible, powerful, and moving. Some mornings I fall asleep as I read. Some mornings I read, pray, go slowly, and remove distractions. At the end, I have no idea what stood out to me or how to apply what I read. That is where the last big idea becomes vital.

Be Consistent

I know the feeling of being excited about spiritual things like reading the Bible, but once I get started, I sometimes feel overwhelmed or lost. I know the feeling of not wanting to be in the Word or doing the things I know I should do. I consistently see others around me who are farther along spiritually, and I feel like I will never be on their level.

Never compare your beginning with someone else's middle or end. This idea of learning to sit and soak in God's Word is a lifetime journey. You never stop learning and growing. If you have little experience, don't compare yourself to someone who has 20 or 40 years of experience.

With that in mind, we must grow in consistency. If you fall off your plan one day, get back in the Word tomorrow. If you fail today, even if it is an epic fail, get back in the Word tomorrow. If you feel

> *Never compare your beginning with someone else's middle or end.*

like it's not working, get back in the Word tomorrow. Whether or not you feel like it, get back into the Word.

The Bible transforms your heart, mind, and soul. God uses it to shape you. Your spiritual growth is usually like watching grass grow. Day to day it feels like nothing is changing. One day you look up, and realize it is time to mow. you need to mow that "grass." As you press into God and dig into His Word, He grows you. I promise. Hebrews 4:12 says, "For the word of God is alive and active. Sharper than any double-edged sword, it penetrates even to dividing soul and spirit, joints and marrow; it judges the thoughts and attitudes of the heart."

You Don't Just Read the Bible; the Bible Reads You. So Dig In.

Think of it like this. God knows everything about you—the good, the bad, and the ugly. And God's heart for you is that He loves you. That's insane, right? He knows me and still loves me!

When we put our faith in God, He accepts us just as we are. We are not too sinful for God to save us. God saves us just as we are. After He saves us, He begins to transform us into who He has called us to be.

> *You don't just read the Bible; the Bible reads you.*

So God gives us His Spirit because He wants us to grow and be close to Him. He gives us the Word of God, prayer, church, and serving to stretch our faith and grow us more and more into His likeness and His image. That is who God is. He really is for us.

As we open up the Word of God tomorrow, we are not reading so God will love us more. We aren't reading because maybe God will owe us something and give us what we want. No, we open the Word because our Father is so good that He has made it possible for us to know Him. As we read His Word, we feel His love and pleasure because we used to be marked by sin but are now marked by His love. As His children, we get to enjoy His presence and His nearness just as He intended when He created the world.

Practice

So what might this look like in real life? I will show you my plan, and then you can create your own.

> *As His children, we get to enjoy His presence and His nearness just as He intended when He created the world.*

Josh's Plan

1. Choose your translation: NIV

2. Create your plan: One chapter a day

   - Time: 5:30

   - Place: Recliner in the living room

   - Distractions that need to be removed: Kids, phone notifications

- How I will read and focus: Physical Bible with pen in hand, underlining as I go

3. Journal or app: Evernote

That's my plan, but don't get caught up in my details. They are just an example. I have been doing this since 2001. I do not have any babies or toddlers in my home anymore. My life is busy, but my days are mostly routine.

The idea is that these suggestions will help you develop a plan for yourself. If it works, make it better. If it doesn't work, try something else. When a new season of life hits, use these suggestions to reevaluate your plan so you can continue to make God a priority.

What is your plan? Fill in the blanks.

1. Choose your translation: _____

   - Create your plan: _____

   - Time: _____

   - Place: _____

   - Distractions that need to be removed:

     _____

   - How I will read and focus:

     _____

2. Journal or app: _____

You can also practice some basic application questions such as "What is the one thing that stood out to me the most and why?" Some passages will speak powerfully, and some will not. That is okay.

Right now, read Psalm 145 *slowly* and mindfully. What stood out to you the most? Why? Write your answers in the blanks below.

_____

_____

_____

_____

Did you stop and read that chapter, or are you skipping the practice to finish this chapter in the book? I am guilty of skipping the practical things when I read books. If you are new to faith or new to reading the Bible, be sure to do the practices so my explanations make sense. It will be helpful.

As I was writing this book, I stopped and read Psalm 145. Verses 13b and 17 stood out to me the most: "The Lord is trustworthy in all he promises and faithful in all he does. The Lord is righteous in all his ways and faithful in all he does."

Why did these verses stick out to me in my current life and season? As I prayerfully pondered that, this came to mind: These verses stand out to me today because there are some things in our community and in my family that seem to show that God isn't faithful and that God isn't trustworthy. Things are happening that I wouldn't choose, and in my limited ability to fathom, they do not make sense to me.

But God's thoughts and His ways are better and higher than mine. I will trust His Word that He is always faithful and forever trustworthy. My circumstances may not feel like that is true, but I will trust God's Word and believe that God is as faithful and trustworthy as the Bible says He is and how He always proves that throughout my life.

Prayer

This book is about the Bible and how to read it. But prayer and Bible reading go hand in hand. Your prayers can be lists. They can be spontaneous. They can be in the form of asking, thanking, praising, and much more. Prayer can be simply sitting in the presence of God in silence with your heart open to God.

I suggest that you learn how to pray Scripture back to God as well. I use prayer in all these forms. Where I tend to start my daily prayers is based on what stood out to me in the text that I read.

For example, in the practice with Psalm 145, my prayers would begin praising God for being trustworthy and faithful. I may even prayerfully remember some of the many ways I have seen His faithfulness firsthand.

My goal is to commune with God through His Word and allow that to lead me into my prayers. Then I go on to lists or specific needs as the season goes.

End

In 2016, my wife had our boys fill out a Father's day question-naire about me. The responses from Gideon were super cute. He is our thirdborn son and was four years old at the time. Callie asked him the questions and then wrote down what he said.

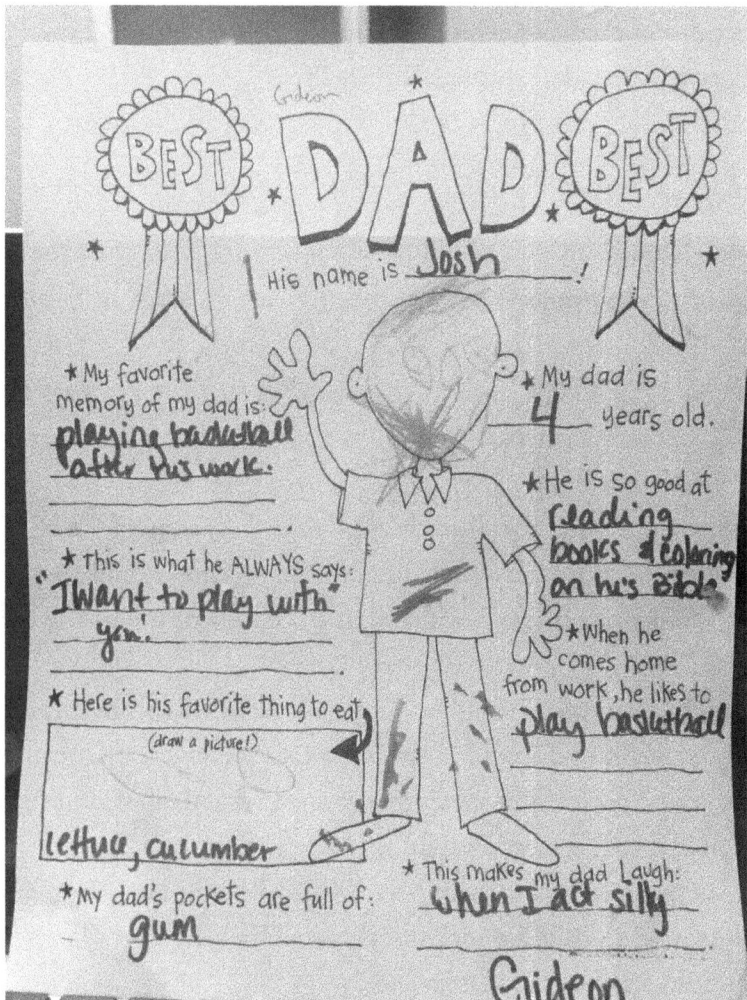

You can see his answers in the picture. Gideon says my favorite sport is playing basketball after work (I am terrible at basketball). My favorite food is lettuce and cucumbers (nope). My pockets are full of gum (gross).

"My dad is 4 years old" (awkward).

Here is the one that brought me to tears. When Callie asked four-year-old Gideon what dad was good at, he said reading books and coloring on his Bible. What he meant by coloring on my Bible was that I read my physical Bible with a pen in hand so I can underline as a I go. In Gideon's four-year-old mind, he just thought I was coloring. But at four years old, he already noticed what I was doing.

One of my deepest hopes is that I will be faithful to the end. I want to be faithful to my God, my wife, and my kids. I also want a genuine faith. I would consider it a failure if my words and beliefs did not line up with my actions. I may be able to fool a church or a world, but my kids would see through me.

I want to leave a legacy that matters. I want to leverage my life for Jesus. I want to live a life of Christian authenticity. I pray that my kids are fully devoted followers of Christ all their days.

I cannot do any of this without learning to soak in God's Word and have it renew and transform my heart, mind, and soul. I wake up most mornings and read the Bible because I am convinced that this book is written by God. I am convinced that God is revealing Himself to me through His Word. I am convinced that if I want to be the Christian, husband, father, friend, and worker that God has called me to be, I must remain close to Him. By God's grace, He has given us His Word so we might know Him.

SMALL GROUP QUESTIONS

1. What is God's heart for His people?

2. Have you ever tried to read the Bible and got caught up simply trying to complete the chapter or the scheduled reading? This chapter said, "Our goal is not to complete a reading plan, but to commune with the living God." How does that go deeper than simply reading the Bible?

3. Did you fill in the blanks in this chapter? If not, please go back and do that, and develop your plan.

4. What do you think will be the easiest part of your plan? What will be the most challenging?

5. Imagine yourself one year from now. What kind of person would you be if you made the principles in this chapter a major priority in your life? What if you practiced these principles for five years? 20? What could God do?

Chapter 8

HOW DO I STUDY THE BIBLE?

My wife is the best cook I know. Praise God from whom all blessings flow. I grew up eating chicken strips and fries at any restaurant I went to, even Mexican restaurants. Over the course of our marriage, my wife has helped me expand my palate. Now I eat things I never dreamed of eating as a child, and I love it all.

Learning to read the Bible devotionally as described in the previous chapter is like a good meal. I love going to a Brazilian steakhouse and eating my weight in various meats and sides. I probably gain 5 pounds every time. This is kind of like reading devotionally. It is an awesome experience, and you benefit greatly. There is so much joy and benefit to be had from it.

It is a deeper experience when you research, gather the ingredients, plan, prepare, cook, and then enjoy a good meal. This chapter is about Bible study, which feels like that. It requires more effort, but it can be incredibly satisfying.

In the last chapter, you only needed your Bible, but you may have to use extra tools to complete this chapter. Using Bible dictionaries, maps, commentaries, online sources, and more will be helpful when you are not sure how to answer some of the suggested questions. Also, there will be passages where you will not be able answer all the questions you may have. That is okay. We want to dig in and learn as much as we can.

Tools You May Need

These are suggestions, not requirements. I will give you some questions and principles throughout this chapter. They may help you more fully answer the questions and understand the principles. All these resources can be found online.

Study Bibles:

- NIV Study Bible
- ESV Study Bible
- NIV Thompson Chain-Reference Bible

Study Bibles give brief commentaries on a passage. They also give cross references and definitions. These three study Bibles have loads of information and extra study in the back. I have used study Bibles on and off for 20 years. Find one you like in the translation you prefer, and then keep it handy.

Reference Books:

- *The Bible Maps Handbook.* This is a little pricey, but it's worth it in my opinion. It lists all 66 books and shows the time they were written, who wrote them, and to whom they were writing. It gives a brief overview of the content of each book. It includes maps and where events took place in the various books of the Bible. This one resource could help you understand the overarching context of every book of the Bible. I keep this book beside my recliner for easy access if I need it.

- *Holman's Illustrated Bible Dictionary.* Many people have preferences for their Bible dictionaries. I encourage you to consider getting one. When looking up definitions of biblical words, using a Bible dictionary is more accurate than a regular dictionary.

- *Strong's Exhaustive Concordance of the Bible.* I first got this in college. It is overwhelming. It indexes every word in the Bible, shows where they are used, and gives definitions. You may not use this every day, but it is good to have it when needed.

Timeline

Search online for "biblical timeline" and find one you like. This is another source that is good to have on hand, so you know where you are in God's grand story. The book of Ezra is the 15th book of the Old Testament. Chronologically, Ezra happens almost at the end of the Old Testament writing. The Bible is not always in chronological order. A timeline helps you focus on where you are in history.

In the rest of this chapter, I will walk you through some overarching ideas and give you a lot of questions to guide you. If you have a study Bible, *The Bible Maps Handbook*, and a timeline, you can answer almost every question and principle I am about to cover.

The three overarching principles are observe, interpret, and apply. Each principle has many questions to guide you.

I am heavily influenced here by the book *Living by the Book* by Howard Hendricks and William Hendricks. The book covers the

> *Observe, interpret, and apply*

three principles (observe, interpret, apply) in detail. This chapter is an oversimplified version of how I have loosely applied this book. If you want to go deeper, I can't recommend a better book.

This chapter takes more effort than the previous chapters, but it is the pathway to unlocking all kinds of insights about God and His Word.

Observe

When you think about digging deeper into the Bible, the best place to start is with observation. This idea is easy to overlook, but it is vitally important. When you read the Bible, it is good to ask as many questions as you can imagine. That means observation is about being inquisitive and curious. The more thoroughly you observe, the more likely your interpretation and application will be biblical, so don't skip this part.

There are two basic layers to observation: listening and looking. I'll quickly walk you through these two ideas, and then we'll practice so you can see them in action.

The idea behind listening is asking questions about the text, context, characters, and more. You may ask something like this:

> *Observation is about being inquisitive and curious.*

- Who wrote the passage? Who was it written to?

- Who are the main characters? What is happening?

- What is the author's purpose?

- Where is the author when they wrote the passage?

- What kind or type of writing is the text (narrative, poetry, history, etc.)? Are there any words or phrases that are repeated?

- Are there any connecting words like *therefore*, *but*, or *for*? Are there any words you do not know or understand?

You can add questions of your own as well. The more questions the better. That means you are being inquisitive.

When we talk about looking at the text, it is the acknowledgment that the Bible is alive and active. You can read the same passage for years and find new things each time. No matter how familiar you are with the text, there is always more to learn.

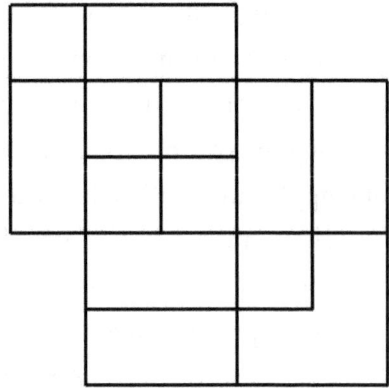

The squares illustration is very helpful here. How many squares do you see?

Honestly, I have no idea how many squares are in this diagram. The more I look at it, the more squares I see. That is what it is like when you observe the Bible. You will always see and learn new things.

Howard Hendricks was famous for having his students at Dallas Theological Seminary do an exercise where they observed Acts 1:8: "But you will receive power when the Holy Spirit comes on you; and you will be my witnesses in Jerusalem, and in all Judea and Samaria, and to the ends of the earth."

He told the students to write 25 different observations from this one verse. There were stories of students agonizing as they tried their hardest to find 25 different observations from one verse. As the story goes, when the students came back to class with their 25 observations, the next assignment was to find 25 new observations from that same verse.

What is fascinating is that the students did it. What is more fascinating is that Professor Hendricks collected over 600 observations of this one verse during his tenure at Dallas Theological Seminary.

The best heart posture is to always come to the Bible with a learning spirit.

Never assume you know what it says or what God wants to do in your life. Always stay curious and inquisitive.

In observation, we are not worried about interpretation or application . . . yet. We just want to ask as many questions and learn as much as we can about the text we are reading.

How many observations can you think of from Acts 1:8? Try to get your own set of 25 observations from this verse.

I also like to use Romans 12:1 and John 15:1–11 for practice. Use the questions above to help. John 15 repeats many words and phrases. Have fun observing it.

Interpret

Being curious and inquisitive is so important, and it launches us into interpretation, which asks what the Bible actually means. What did the original writers mean?

Not to be repetitive, but this is so important to review again. God is the main character of the Bible. The Bible is one big story of the lengths God is willing to go to

> *Interpretation asks what the Bible actually means. What did the original writers mean?*

rescue and redeem mankind. Christ is the hero, not us. When we are studying the Bible, the more we understand this big story, the more accurate we will interpret the immediate text we are studying.

The Old Testament points to Jesus. The Gospels (Matthew, Mark, Luke, and John) tell about the life, death, burial, and resurrection of Jesus. Acts teaches how the church spread all over the world in the first century. Romans to Revelation tell us about what Jesus has done and how we, the church, live in light of that, knowing He will return one day.

If this is true, and I am banking my life on that, then it helps shape the questions we ask when we are trying to interpret the text.

Before we move on to helpful questions, I want to warn you what not to do. Do not ask, "What does this passage mean to me?" A passage can mean something to me that the Bible never intends it to mean. This is a dangerous question because it can lead people to believe the Bible is approving of behavior or beliefs that the Bible has never taught.

Our heart posture is not to assume a belief or a truth and then try to make the Bible prove what we think is true. Rather, we want to humbly come to the Bible and

> *Do not ask, "What does this passage mean to me?"*

allow it to teach us what is true and right. We want to be obsessed to do everything in our power to interpret the Bible according to what the original writers intended, not what we want to force the Bible to say.

In order to do that, I use four questions when trying to more fully understand a text.

- Where and how does this passage fit into the whole story?
- What does this text teach about God?
- What does this text teach about mankind?
- What does this text teach about Jesus?

Where and how does this passage fit into the whole story? Abraham never met Joseph, Joseph never met David, and David never met Nehemiah. None of these people ever met Peter. The Bible takes place over thousands of years. It is very helpful to understand where the passage takes place and how it fits into the story.

I love biblical timelines. They can help you quickly clarify where you are in the middle of God's grand story. You can easily find them online.

What is also fascinating to me is that some of the characters do overlap. Joshua is Moses's assistant. Moses dies, and then Joshua leads the people into the Promised Land as told in the book of Joshua. It seems that Ezekiel, Daniel, and Jeremiah were all alive and writing during the same time period. Jesus's brothers seem to be against Jesus during his life. But after His resurrection, they become bold leaders in the church. The book of James is written by Jesus's half-brother. The more you study, the more you learn details like this.

What does the text teach about God? If God is the main character, we should be looking at the text with Him first and foremost in our minds. We will be tempted to read ourselves into many passages, but it is most helpful to start with God if we are going to understand the original intentions.

We also grow more and more into God's likeness and image as we behold Him (2 Cor. 3:18). When reading the Bible, we want to see God's nature, character, and qualities. We are looking to see how God acts and behaves. We are looking for what God cares about and what God hates. The more we know God, the more it shapes and changes us from the inside out. What is the Bible trying to teach us about the nature and character of God?

What does the text teach about mankind? The temptation is to make us the hero when Jesus is the hero of the story. The Bible is so honest about our sin, needs, and the true state of our hearts and minds. It also teaches us about how

> *When reading the Bible, we want to see God's nature, character, and qualities.*

life is best lived. As we read and study, we want to be honest about what it says about mankind, both in the positive and negative ways.

What does the text teach about Jesus? Some passages explicitly teach about Jesus. Some are more layered and vague. We are in the story of God, but the climax is Jesus and His gospel. We are living in light of that overarching story. This question is good because it keeps the gospel in the forefront of our minds.

There is one more caveat I want to discuss. There are parts of the Bible that are very difficult to understand. The smartest and most godly people in the world interpret them differently.

Generically speaking, when you come to a difficult passage, use the filter questions in this chapter, and do the best you can. Also, a basic rule of Bible interpretation is that the Bible interprets the Bible. If you are studying a passage that seems to contradict another passage of Scripture, assume you are the problem, not the Bible. As we discussed in Chapters 1 and 2, God wrote the Word. He made no mistakes. It does not contradict.

Historically, there have been people who have argued that Romans 3:28 and James 2:24 contradict each other.

> *The Bible interprets the Bible.*

- Romans 3:28 says, "For we maintain that a person is justified by faith apart from the works of the law."

- James 2:24 says, "You see that a person is considered righteous by what they do and not by faith alone."

A simple reading of just those verses seems to show a blatant contradiction. But when you apply the questions and principles of this chapter, you will see that in the context of the verses, both authors' intents are perfectly in line with each other.

Again, the four questions in this section are not the only questions you can and should ask when trying to discern an author's original intent. They are a framework to help you learn how to properly understand a text you are reading. The more we can understand the author's original intent, the more accurate we can then apply the text, which is the next principle.

Apply

The third and final principle of study is application. This is thinking through how we respond to what the Word of God says and means. This is important because to refuse to apply the Scripture tends to create self-righteousness. Just knowing the Scriptures is never the goal. We want to know the God of the Scriptures. The Scriptures lead us to God's heart. To know the Bible but not have God's heart tends to create religious, pharisaical, and hard-hearted people.

The texts in the Bible have one interpretation. They mean what the author intended for them to mean. Every verse has one interpretation but many applications.

I always find it helpful to prayerfully ask God for the one verse, phrase, or idea that stands out to me the most. Let's go a little further in this section.

When you think about applying the Word, you need to think about more than just actions.

Every verse has one interpretation but many applications.

When I first began digging into the Word, I associated application with doing. This is true, but it is not the only way you can apply Scripture. Application can be to inform, challenge, correct, encourage and more.

This could be in the form of action, something you do or stop doing. It could also be in the form of belief. Maybe you believe something falsely or maybe you are believing a lie that the Bible rebukes. Application can also be standing in awe of who God is and what He has done.

I want to show you how we can apply one verse in these various ways. Look at Ephesians 4:32: "Be kind and compassionate to one another, forgiving each other, just as in Christ God forgave you."

Application can be to inform, challenge, correct, encourage, and more.

Application can be an action, or a belief, or it can lead us to stand in awe. How can Ephesians 4:32 lead to an action?

When you are reading this verse, the Holy Spirit may remind you of someone you have not forgiven. For the believer, forgiving others is a command, not a suggestion. Biblically, it doesn't say forgive if you feel like it. Your response to this text could be that you send a text, make a phone call, or talk to someone in person where you verbally tell them you forgive them. These are action-oriented applications.

How can the application of this verse be a belief? Some people are rude to people and justify it by saying, "That's just my personality. That is just the way I am." No, it isn't. You are choosing to be unkind and to lack compassion.

If you are a believer, we are called to step into love, kindness, and compassion with others the same way Jesus did. It is a lie to believe that you are just made that way when that way is against the Bible. That is a lie to rebuke.

How can the application of this verse lead us to stand in awe? It says to forgive one another just as in Christ God forgave you. How much did God forgive you for? Everything? Does that challenge your heart? The God of the universe knows everything about you and was still willing to lay down His life so you might have life now and forever. The realization that God was willing to die for you should lead you to awe, praise, adoration, surrender, and much more.

Every verse has one interpretation, but every verse has an untold number of applications—not just three. We could all read the same verse or passage, and the Spirit might speak to all of us differently.

Let's practice some more. Go back to the other verses we have used so far. Use the questions from observation and interpretation on Romans 12:1, John 15:1–11, and the Romans 2:28 and James 2:24 "controversy." Answer as many of these questions as you can:

- Who wrote the passage? Who was it written to?

- Who are the main characters? What is happening?

- What is the author's purpose?

- Where is the author when they wrote the passage?

- What kind or type of writing is the text (narrative, poetry, history, etc.)? Are there any words or phrases that are repeated?

- Are there any connecting words such as *therefore*, *but*, or *for*? Are there any words you do not know or understand?

- Where and how does this passage fit into the whole story? What does this text teach about God?

- What does this text teach about mankind?

- What does this text teach about Jesus?

- How do these passages lead you to act, believe, or stand in awe of God?

The Word is alive and active. You will never get to a point where you have nothing to learn from the Bible. God is always speaking to us through His Word.

The more you read and get familiar with the Bible and the big story, the more it makes sense. The more it makes sense, the more you learn how to observe, interpret, and apply it. The more you learn how to do this, the more you learn about the nature and character of God. The more you know about God, the more you stand in awe of who He is and what He has done.

I can think of no better habit to form than the habit of daily communing with God through His Word and prayer. Let's pursue Him like never before. He is worth it.

1. If you do not have all the reference materials listed at the beginning of this chapter, don't worry. I suggest borrowing some of them or buying just one to try it out. As you develop, you will know what you need the most. What one thing might you consider pursuing first?

2. Explain each of these terms: observe, interpret, and apply.

3. Read Acts 1:8. Can you get 10 observations? 25?

4. What is the one question the author warns you not to use in interpretation?

5. There is one interpretation of a passage, but many. What are potential ways you can apply passages of Scripture?

CONCLUSION

My heart and hope is that this book is helpful. I want you to have a lot of trust in God's Word. It is written by God, and it is for us. I want you to know the overarching story of the Bible. Basic Bible literacy is vital to our spiritual growth. Most of all, I want you to learn how to commune with the living God through the Word He has chosen to give us. By our very design, God's heart is that He wants us to know Him. What a privilege we have!

With this in mind, I want to reiterate one principle one last time. Spiritual growth often feels slow. Reading the Bible can feel like it's not working. It can feel like a waste of time. It can feel like you will never learn the content or how to read it in a beneficial way.

Through all these "feels," keep pressing on and moving forward. Don't stop pursuing God through His Word, especially in seasons where God feels distant, or the Word feels dry. This happens in the life of the believer. In dry spiritual seasons, the best choice is to worship through it, not avoid it.

Pursue God through the Word, prayer, and worship. Trust

that God is speaking and moving even when you can't see it. Choose what is right regardless of how you feel.

Lastly, get excited. If you put the principles of this book into daily practice, you will grow. I can say that confidently, not because I trust this book but because this book pushes me to the Book. You will grow because God's Word grows, shapes, corrects, encourages, and informs you. As you grow, God will use you.

When the Word of Christ dwells in you richly, the Word of God will overflow and spill out onto others. The result is not just that we grow spiritually but that everyone around us benefits from our life that is becoming more and more like Christ. Praise be to God!

Get to it. Make a plan. Try it out. If it works, make it better. If it doesn't work, fix it. Read slowly. Read mindfully. Allow the Scriptures to form your prayers. Commune with the living God. Above all, don't stop. Keep coming back to the fountain of God's Word, and allow Him to refresh your soul.

ENDNOTES

1. Cru. "How It Came to Be: A Brief History of the Bible." *Cru*. Accessed May 21, 2025. https://www.cru.org/us/en/train-and-grow/bible-studies/how-it-came-to-be-a-brief-history-of-the-bible.html.

2. Mark Driscoll and Gerry Breshears, *Doctrine: What Christians Should Believe* (Wheaton, IL: Crossway, 2010), 47–48

3. Paul Gibson, "How Does the Quantity of New Testament Manuscripts Compare to Other Ancient Manuscripts?" *Bible Questions.info*, December 14, 2019, https://biblequestions.info/2019/12/14/how-does-the-quantity-of-new-testament-manuscripts-compare-to-other-ancient-manuscripts/.

4. "Biblical Manuscripts," Dunham Bible Museum, Houston Christian University, https://hc.edu/museums/dunham-bible-museum/tour-of-the-museum/past-exhibits/biblical-manuscripts/.

5. A free online version of the entire book *Science Speaks* is available at https://sciencespeaks.dstoner.net/index.html#c0.

6. David R. Reagan, "Applying the Science of Probability to the Scriptures," *Lamb & Lion Ministries*, https://christinprophecy.org/articles/ applying-the-science-of-probability-to-the-scriptures/.

7. Michael J. Kruger, "The Biblical Canon," *TGS*, https://www.the gospelcoalition.org/essay/the-biblical-canon/.

8. Flavuis Josephus, *Against Apion*, 1.42.

9. Mike McGarry, "The Canonicity of the Bible: Five Apologetics Every Student Needs," *Rooted*, February 23, 2016, https://rooted ministry.com/five-apologetics-every-student-needs-the-canonicity-of-the-bible/?gad_source=1&gbraid=0AAAAACVWTBs5 sh0dKNYbyhZEPfmwU8vlj&gclid=Cj0KCQjww-HABh CGARIsALLO6Xx194RL3Un_G7S9VCJDPtHWZW1rB du6mCV43TPdZXSm9150Z9clSQYaAs08EALw_wcB.

10. Wayne Grudem, *Systematic Theology* (Zondervan Academic, 1994), Chapter 3.

11. Wayne Grudem, *Systematic Theology* (Zondervan Academic, 1994), 515.